THE ESSENTIAL GUIDE TO EFFECTIVE CORPORATE BOARD COMMITTEES

THE ESSENTIAL GUIDE
TO EFFECTIVE
CORPORATE BOARD
COMMITTEES

LOUIS BRAIOTTA, JR.
School of Management
University Center at Binghamton
State University of New York

A. A. SOMMER, JR.
Morgan, Lewis & Bockius
Counselors at Law

Prentice-Hall, Inc., *Englewood Cliffs, New Jersey 07632*

Library of Congress Cataloging-in-Publication Data

Braiotta, Louis, date.
The essential guide to effective corporate
board committees.

Includes index.
1. Directors of corporations. 2. Management
committees. I. Sommer, A. A. (Alphonse A.),
1924– . II. Title.
HD2745.B63 1987 658.4'22 87–2265
ISBN 0-13-286139-9

To my daughter Elena and my family
—L.B.

Editorial/production supervision and
  interior design: Madelaine Cooke
Cover design: Edsal Enterprises
Manufacturing buyer: Carol J. Bystrom

© 1987 by Prentice-Hall, Inc.
A Division of Simon & Schuster
Englewood Cliffs, New Jersey 07632

Printed in the United States of America

10 9 8 7 6 5 4 3 2 1

ISBN 0-13-286139-9 025

Prentice-Hall International (UK) Limited, *London*
Prentice-Hall of Australia Pty. Limited, *Sydney*
Prentice-Hall Canada Inc., *Toronto*
Prentice-Hall Hispanoamericana, S.A., *Mexico*
Prentice-Hall of India Private Limited, *New Delhi*
Prentice-Hall of Japan, Inc., *Tokyo*
Prentice-Hall of Southeast Asia Pte. Ltd., *Singapore*
Editora Prentice-Hall do Brasil, Ltda., *Rio de Janeiro*

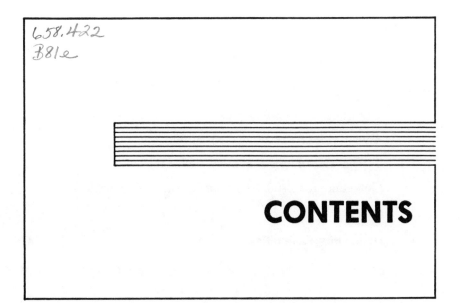

CONTENTS

Preface   **ix**

Foreword   **xi**

I   BOARD COMMITTEES AND THE CORPORATE ENVIRONMENT

1   The Renewed Interest in Boards of Directors   **1**
     Historical Development   3
     The Aftermath of Watergate   6

2   The Law of Board Committees   **21**
     General Principles   23
     Power of the Board to Appoint Committees   25
     The Appointment of Committees   28
     Reliance by Non-Committee Members   29
     Duties of Committee Members   32

II BOARD COMMITTEES IN ACTION

3   Executive Committees   **37**

Historical Development   39

Advantages of Executive Committees   40

Typical Committee Functions   42

Guidelines for Establishing an Executive Committee   44

4   Nominating Committees   **47**

Historical Development   49

Importance of Nominating Committees   49

Responsibilities of Nominating Committees   51

5   Compensation Committees   **61**

Historical Development   63

Benefits of Compensation Committees   63

Characteristics of a Compensation Committee's Task   66

An Illustrative Discussion of Executive Compensation   69

6   Public-Policy Committees   **75**

Historical Development   77

Significance of Pubic-Policy Committees   77

Operational Aspects of Public-Policy Committees   79

7   Finance Committees   **85**

Historical Development   87

Need for Finance Committees   88

Basic Committee Structure and Functions   88

8   Audit Committees   **95**

Historical Development   97

Audit Committee Organization   98

Committee Meetings and Agenda Items   101

9   Special Committees   **111**

Historical Development and Court Actions   113

Litigation Committees   118

Investigating Committees   121

Acquisition Committees   122

Other Special Committees   125

III   BOARD COMMITTEE REPORTS

10   Reporting to the Board   **127**

Definition and Importance of Committee Reports   129

Preparation of Committee Reports   130

CONCLUDING OBSERVATIONS   **137**

APPENDICES

A   Foreign Corrupt Practices Act   139

B   Proactive Position on Corporate Accountability and
     Board Committee Structure   144

C   Committees of the Board   148

D   Revised Model Business Corporation Act—Chapter 8:
     Directors and Officers   150

E   Section 182 of the Business Corporation Act—Ontario,
     Canada   163

F   Business Conduct Guidelines   164

G   Management's Financial Responsibility   171

H   Business or Professional Organizations and Directors
     Publications   173

Index   **175**

PREFACE

The role and responsibilities of corporate board committees in the United States continue to receive increasing attention in both the public and private sectors because of the demands for greater corporate accountability. Board committees are mechanisms through which the full board of directors can provide responsible corporate governance. Several published studies have found that a number of individual corporations have established several board committees in order to assure the full board that management fulfills its responsibilities in the interests of the stockholders and other constituencies of the corporation. Therefore, the notion that the board of directors performs a "rubber stamp" function is clearly false in light of the board's initiatives to establish standing committees.

The purpose of this book is to serve the needs of corporate board committee members. The book is designed to explain what appropriate actions may be taken to make board committees more effective. For directors, executives, and others who interact with board committees, the book offers guidance and information for the development of constructive relationships between each standing committee and the full board of directors, management, and other external parties, such as external auditors and outside consultants. The book is organized to provide a balance between a conceptual presentation of the functions of individual board committees and an understandable presentation of practical ideas to aid active committee members.

Part 1, "Board Committees and the Corporate Environment," covers the renewed interest in boards of directors and the law of board committees.

Part 2, "Board Committees in Action," provides a discussion relative to special committees, the executive committee, the nominating committee, the compensation committee, the public-policy committee, the finance committee, and the audit committee.

Part 3, "Board Committee Reports," covers the reporting function of the board committees and discusses guidelines for preparing committee reports.

In sum, this book seeks to provide helpful guidance to make board committees more effective.

LOUIS BRAIOTTA, JR.
A. A. SOMMER, JR.

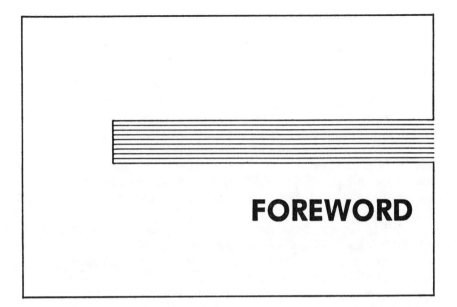

FOREWORD

The desirability of "outside," or "independent," directors on the boards of publicly held companies is no longer disputed. Even though the increase in their numbers may be temporarily slowed by liability and insurance developments, there can be little doubt that their presence and their influence will continue to grow in the years to come.

It is not enough, however, that these directors be accepted and that they serve. They must be given the means, the opportunity, and the structure with which they can also be *effective*.

The best independent directors are usually employed full time in the high office of another corporation, or have a governmental or academic position of high responsibility, or in other ways have demands upon their time. Thus, corporations wishing to maximize the contribution outside directors can make must adopt whatever means may be available to facilitate their participation and conserve their time and energies.

There are many ways of doing this. Carefully prepared reports, both written and oral, to the directors can do much to permit them to grasp quickly and surely the problems of the company they serve. Careful selection of the matters to come before the board is helpful too.

However, no better device than board committees provides the potential for meaningful and effective participation by board members. Through these committees board members may probe into important areas of corporate concern more deeply than would be possible in a full board meeting. In the audit committee a company's directors may consider in greater depth the contents of the company's financial statements, the adequacy of its internal controls, and the integrity of its disclosures. Notwithstanding the accepted importance of the audit committee in the scheme of corporate governance, recent research suggests that among medium and smaller companies an audit committee is often still not seen as an essential tool of responsible corporate governance. The result is that many such companies do not have audit committees, and many of those that do have such committees fail to realize their potential: Meetings are infrequent, unstructured, and essentially meaningless.

While not having achieved the importance of audit committees, nominating and compensation committees have been steadily growing in importance. In the eyes of many the nominating committee may be the key to boards of directors that are dominated by truly independent directors. Where responsible nominating committees exist, "cronyism" as the entranceway to the boardroom disappears, and a greater emphasis is placed upon the unique talents, experience, and skills that potential board members may bring to the directors' table. It is not utopian to expect that as nominating committees mature they will increasingly assume the admittedly unpleasant task of assessing performance of board members and by counseling and, ultimately, denial of renomination compel a steady strengthening of boards.

If the predictions of many commentators are true that present United States corporate compensation practices are due for a critical reappraisal, compensation committees will assume much greater importance. The day is past when a compensation committee acted simply as a rubber stamp for management's recommendations. Increasingly, on the positive side, it must assure that the compensation practices of its company are such as to entice and keep the human talent without which no business can succeed. On the negative side, it must assure that a management that has compiled a mediocre or poor record sees a reflection of that in its compensation. Most compensation committees have not yet realized their responsibility in this regard.

Many corporations, particularly larger ones, having witnessed the success of the more common and conventional committees, have developed additional committees to deal with particular areas. Public affairs committees, environmental committees, ethics committees, and a host of others have been created as an economical and efficient means of providing input to management with regard to sensitive and important areas. And, of course, the so-called "special," or "litigation," committee, usually born of a crisis within the corporation or serious charges against management, has proven a valuable instrument in times of intense corporate stress. As their responsibility and independence are further evidenced, these committees will be accorded by the courts greater leeway in dealing conclusively with the matters they confront.

It is axiomatic now that a "critical mass" of outside directors is essential for the board of any publicly held company. However, directors independent of management do not simply by their presence assure the benefits they should provide. Only if their talents, their energies, their experience, and their strengths are mobilized and channeled can their potential be realized. Strong, well-organized, well-oriented, and conscientious committees are the best means found yet to assure maximum benefits from boards. As the first book to deal extensively with these important matters, *The Essential Guide to Effective Corporate Board Committees* is an important contribution to the growing literature about boards of directors.

HAROLD M. WILLIAMS
President and Chief Executive Officer,
The J. Paul Getty Trust (former chairman,
Securities and Exchange Commission; former
dean, Graduate School of Management,
University of California at Los Angeles)

1

RENEWED INTEREST
IN BOARDS
OF DIRECTORS

HISTORICAL DEVELOPMENT

In recent years there has been a steadily increasing interest in the role of boards of directors in modern American corporations, both those for profit and those that are nonprofit. This interest has evoked great discussion, not only in business circles but throughout society. The discussion of this has embraced many questions: How big should a board be? What should its composition be? How many "inside" directors and "outside" directors should a board have? What is the proper role of a board? How should board members be compensated? What should the responsibilities of a board be? What liabilities should be imposed on board members? How should a board be organized?

These by no means exhaust the questions that may be asked concerning boards of directors. The last question—how should a board be organized—is the focus of this book. The answer to that question depends on the answers to a host of others. If a board is perceived as largely a figurehead, with little real power and no expectation that it will have significant influence on the affairs of the corporation, there is little need for structuring the board with committees. On the other hand, as the responsibilities and expectations of a board grow, committees are possible components of a structure designed to provide greater efficiency in carrying out board functions, which becomes increasingly necessary as a board consists of greater numbers of outsiders whose time available for board business is usually sharply limited.

This increased concern with directors and their roles and responsibilities is the result of considerable history that explains in some measure this concern and emphasis.

Corporations have a long history in English and United States common law (the law of every commercial society has provision for some sort of entity, known by various names, that is essentially a corporation). Scholars have long debated whether corporations originated with the voluntary bandings together of persons seeking a common goal—for instance, members of a guild—or whether they were originally creations of the sovereign. Regardless of the historical seed, by the time the North American colonies were established, corporations came into existence by act of the sovereign. Today that notion is preserved in the laws of all the states, which provide for incorporation under their respective laws.

Early corporations were authorized by royal or legislative act. Those enactments generally laid out in specific detail limitations on the activities of the corporation: The business in which it could engage was spelled out, and it could engage in no other; its duration was typically limited; the amount of capital it could have was also limited. Acts done outside the limits of the specific charter were null and void.

The necessity of specific legislative action to create a corporation understandably fostered a strong link between government and business: Securing a charter became a matter of persuading legislative leaders to grant the valuable franchise. This link between business and government bred people's first suspicion of business, a suspicion that has waxed and waned in intensity from Colonial times to the present. Those early Americans, having witnessed and shaken loose from abuses of power, were wary of power and those who possessed it—the Constitution and its initial expositor, the Federalist papers, are suffused with this wariness—and they saw seeds of troubles in this strengthening alliance of government and business.

As the pace of business enterprise quickened during the Industrial Revolution, the practice of doling out charters one by one became burdensome. Beginning in the late eighteenth century, states began adopting laws permitting incorporations for the purpose of engaging in specific businesses—for example, the development and operation of canals—without a specifically enacted charter. Early in the nineteeth century the first *general corporation laws* were enacted. These laws permitted incorporation without specific legislative action for virtually any lawful purpose; however, these statutes continued to circumscribe closely the activities of corporations incorporated under them. They could engage only in the activities stated in their charters; they could issue only securities authorized in the charter; they could not own stock in other corporations; shareholders' and creditors' rights were protected with a network of limitations on what the corporation could and could not do. This was the prevailing pattern until late in the century when some states, notably New Jersey and, later, Delaware, removed the strictures that had previously limited the prerogatives of corporations. Thus, corporations became able to own stock in other corporations (opening the door to *holding companies*), nonvoting stock was permitted, purposes could be more broadly stated, and acceptance of property and services for stock was permitted. The stage was set for the debate that has endured until now concerning the proper roles and powers of corporations.

In early corporations, directors were selected from among the shareholders to direct the enterprise. Typically they were not paid, because their stake as shareholders in the enterprise was considered a sufficient inducement for them to protect the interests of all shareholders. The practice of directors' being significant shareholders who received no special compensation continued through most of the nineteenth century and well into the twentieth.

The population's suspicion of power, political and economic, has extended to corporations as such, which from time to time have been perceived as abusing the privileges accorded them by the states. This perception has varied in intensity, depending upon events. Typically, in wartime and in times of prosperity and economic growth, businesspersons are heroes and role models; during other times, particularly times of depression, panic, and unemployment, they are seen as villains, and proposals to harness their power come to the surface in quantity.

The latter part of the nineteenth century witnessed great expansion in the size of enterprises. To some extent this was the consequence of the more permissive corporation laws enacted during that time (it was no accident that the original Standard Oil Company was incorporated in New Jersey, which was the first "mother of corporations"). These more liberal laws were responsive to the needs of those in business and legislators alike. The fusing of the nation into a single economic unit demanded larger enterprises, and these new giants needed a new kind of legal structure. Thus came into existence the holding companies and "goliaths" that stirred deep and passionate hostility.

As a consequence of the fears generated by these behemoths, the Sherman Antitrust Act was adopted in an attempt to curb their burgeoning power.

While the debate over the proper structure of business corporations continued into the twentieth century, it was somewhat in abeyance through World War I and the explosive economy of the 1920s but burst into full vigor again with the collapse of 1929 and the subsequent revelations of corporate venality and abuse. This gave rise to the reforms of the New Deal, including the Securities Act of

1933 and the Securities Exchange Act of 1934, which sought to reform certain practices of corporations and the markets in which their securities were traded.

Not long after these reforms were in place came World War II and the incredible accomplishments of United States business in providing the arms needed to defeat Germany and Japan. That triumph for business was followed by the prosperity of the 1950s and early 1960s.

As expansion slowed, voices critical of United States business, which had been largely muted, again were heard. As concerns about the environment, worker safety, consumer protection, and other social problems claimed the stage, business again came under attack as the primary source of the ills of the country.

While these matters mounted, a new and more dramatic trauma afflicted the business community: the disclosures that are sometimes characterized as the "corporate Watergate." This was initially the revelation by the special prosecutor appointed to investigate the "political Watergate" that a number of United States corporations had illegally contributed to the 1972 campaign of President Nixon. The Securities and Exchange Commission (SEC) followed up these disclosures with a number of investigations that discovered not only illegal political contributions but other extensive misconduct, principally improper payments in connection with business done overseas, often paid from accounts maintained off the corporate books.

Related to the events of Watergate in time, and perhaps in popular perception, were other events in the corporate world that further tarnished the reputation of business in the United States. Principal among these were the failures of several substantial companies, failures accompanied in many instances by suggestions that managements may have been guilty of chicanery leading to the failures. In connection with those events, there were frequent charges that auditors had not done their jobs properly and had by their lack of diligence contributed to the misleading of investors.

THE AFTERMATH OF WATERGATE

The disclosures in the wake of Watergate triggered the most intensive study and discussion of United States corporate governance, including the role and responsibilities of directors, yet undertaken.

Among those who became involved were both houses of Congress, several federal agencies (most notably the SEC), the administration, innumerable scholars, and business and professional groups (including the Business Roundtable, the American Bar Association, and the American Institute of Certified Public Accountants).

Out of all this concern and activity flowed a substantial body of judge-made law, the Foreign Corrupt Practices Act,[1] and a number of other legislative proposals that did not pass; increased disclosure requirements imposed by the SEC, some of which, interestingly, have already been modified; a moderate additional involvement of the New York Stock Exchange in corporate governance; considerable change in the composition and organization of boards; and a continuing concern in many quarters about the problem of corporate governance and corporate accountability.

Because the SEC has loomed as the largest player on this field, let us first examine its role.

First, it should be noted that the commission's attention to the conduct of directors, and the subject of corporate accountability and governance generally, antedated the corporate Watergate. In the early 1970s, following the bankruptcy of Penn Central, the commission undertook a comprehensive study of that collapse[2] and subsequently sued various persons involved in it, including three outside directors (the first instance in which the SEC sued anyone whose sole connection with the wrongdoer was service as an outside director). In its report of the study and in its suit, the commission strongly criticized the inattention and indifference of the directors toward the affairs of the company—their failure to make meaningful inquiries, their excessive reliance on representations of officers, and their undue passivity.

In its report on the Penn Central collapse to a congressional committee, the staff of the SEC stated that the Penn Central board

> failed in two principal ways. It failed to establish procedures, including a flow of adequate financial information, to permit the board to understand what was happening and to enable it to exercise some control over the conduct of the senior officers. Secondly, the board failed to respond to specific warnings about the true condition of the com-

[1]See Appendix A for more information.

[2]*The Financial Collapse of the Penn Central Company*, Staff Report of the Securities and Exchange Commission, Washington D.C., August 1972.

pany and about the questionable conduct of the most important officers. As a result, the investors were deprived of adequate and accurate information about the condition of the company.[3]

Beginning in 1974, the commission's concerns reflected in Penn Central were repeatedly expressed, not only in Watergate-originated cases but in others as well. In a number of them, the commission expressed its belief that directors had been inactive, too indifferent, too lacking in attention to the conduct of management. But it was not in the charges that the commission had its greatest impact, but rather in the settlements that they exacted from defendants in these actions. Under the creative and imaginative leadership of Stanley Sporkin, who during this period was the SEC director of enforcement, the commission staff negotiated settlements that conveyed an unmistakable message about the commission's beliefs concerning the structures and standards that should characterize appropriate corporate governance.

Repeatedly the staff insisted upon settlements that included the addition of outside directors to boards, in some cases introducing such to a board for the first time; the creation of audit committees composed exclusively of outside directors; and the organization of special committees to investigate the commission's beliefs that misconduct had occurred.

In one case the commission described in detail the duties that an audit committee to be created pursuant to the settlement should assume.[4] The committee was, inter alia, to monitor closely the financial reports of the company and to maintain close liaison with the company's auditors; to have the power to investigate matters brought to its attention; to report on its activities to the board; to review press releases and communications with shareholders; to review activities of officers and directors with respect to the company; and to monitor the code of conduct of the company.

These enforcement actions and settlements did more than simply impose upon the defendants mandates as to board composition and organization. They signaled to the corporate community the commission's concerns and its suggested remedies for those concerns. Not surprisingly, many companies not immediately menaced by the com-

[3]Ibid., p. 153.

[4]SEC v. Killearn Properties, Inc. (77–78 Transfer Binder, Commerce Clearing House, Federal Securities Law Reporter, par. 96256, N.D. Fla. 1977).

mission took to heart these concerns and remedies and voluntarily undertook a revamp of their boards.

Notwithstanding the commission's aggressive stance in making settlements, it should be borne in mind that these settlements grew out of complaints alleging no more than failures to make proper disclosure. The commission has no power to impose or even to seek sanctions for directorial or managerial misconduct unless it is related to disclosure deficiencies; similarly it has no power to impose corporate governance reforms upon a defendant unilaterally. The novelty in its post-Watergate settlements was the development through negotiation (some say intimidation) of procedural and structural corporate reforms designed to assure a continuing commitment to proper accountability and governance.

The second means used by the commission to influence boards was its historical tool, disclosure. It expanded the information required in documents disseminated to shareholders about directors' and officers' relationships and dealings with the company; the existence, constitution, duties, and frequency of meeting of committees (an earlier proposal that would have in effect prescribed the duties of committees was withdrawn after a storm of criticism); the regularity of attendance by directors at meetings of the board and committees; and a variety of less important details.[5]

While the commission insisted that these disclosure requirements were consistent with the commission's historical role of assuring investors and shareholders timely and accurate information important to them in making investment and voting decisions, it does not strain the imagination to suggest that the commission may have hoped and expected that these additional disclosures would inhibit conflict relationships between corporations and their directors and encourage the organization of committees mainly consisting of "independent" directors.

A third means used by the commission to influence corporate governance practices was "jaw-boning." Chairmen and commissioners repeatedly addressed the duties and responsibilities of directors, their role in corporate governance, and the necessity for a heightened sense of accountability on the part of corporations. Through this means the commission sought to communicate to the

[5]Securities and Exchange Commission, Division of Corporation Finance, *Staff Report on Corporate Accountability*, Washington, D.C., 1980.

corporate world its perception of these matters, even though its statutory mandate to reform corporate practices was a minimal and sharply defined one.

During this period, no one spoke more frequently or more thoughtfully of such matters than Harold M. Williams, SEC chairman from 1977 to 1981. He is perhaps best remembered for his January 1978 proposal that the ideal board should have only one inside director who should be the chief executive officer but who should not chair the board.[6] Interestingly, in August 1984, Harold Geneen, a former chairman of ITT, Inc., not previously perceived as a corporate reformer, took Williams's proposal a step further by suggesting that the ideal board should have *no* inside directors.[7]

However, Williams's concerns went beyond this proposal, and he repeatedly spoke of the responsibilities of directors, both generally and in specific contexts, such as tender offers.

In 1977 the commission organized the Task Force on Corporate Accountability. This staff task force held hearings in Washington, New York, Los Angeles, and Chicago. In September 1980 it published its report, which analyzed the full gamut of corporate governance and accountability issues and made numerous recommendations for reform, none of which was far-reaching or unusually innovative. A central theme was the urging upon corporate leadership of the changes outlined lest they or worse be legislatively imposed.[8]

The task force concluded, as would be expected, that a board should include at least a majority of genuinely independent directors and that publicly held companies should have functioning, effective auditing, nominating, and compensation committees. It suggested that if the trend toward the establishment of audit committees faltered, the commission should perhaps consider mandating such committees. With respect to nominating committees, the task force suggested that if companies did not disclose sufficient information regarding the criteria for selecting nominees for directors and the procedures for making nominations, the commission should consider amending the proxy rules to require the disclosure of such information.

[6]BNA Sec. Reg. L. Rept., No. 437, Jan. 25, 1978, p. A-22.
[7]Harold Geneen, *Managing* (New York: Avon, 1984), p. 268.
[8]Ibid., n. 4.

The events associated with the corporate Watergate understandably triggered interest in both houses of Congress. This congressional interest manifested itself in several ways.

The only legislative achievement that eventuated was the Foreign Corrupt Practices Act, which was enacted in 1977.[9] This statute had two thrusts: First, it made illegal certain payments to foreign governmental and party officials in connection with securing or retaining business abroad; second, it made it illegal for a reporting company to fail to maintain an adequate system of internal controls or to fail to maintain proper books, records, and accounts.

Other, more far-reaching legislation was also proposed. In 1980 Congressman Benjamin Rosenthal and several colleagues and Senator Howard Metzenbaum introduced legislation intended to federalize extensively the rules with respect to the manner in which corporations are governed, as well as to subject corporations to other new and, particularly in the case of Congressman Rosenthal's bill, stringent restrictions.[10]

While neither of these bills went beyond introduction, their provisions, particularly as they relate to boards and committees, are interesting.

The Rosenthal bill, which was largely patterned after proposals suggested by Ralph Nader and his colleagues in *Taming the Giant Corporation*, stated in its preamble that it was a bill "to develop a system of self-governance for large corporations that increases the participation of shareholders and directors in company decision-making. . . ." Among its findings were that

> the system of State chartering of national and multinational corporations is archaic and totally ineffective as a mechanism for accomplishing the purpose of effective corporation governance [and] shareholders and directors are generally excluded from the meaningful participation in the decision-making processes of large corporations.[11]

The bill was intended to apply, with certain limited exceptions, only to United States corporations in manufacturing, mining, retail-

[9]The act is contained in Title I of Public Law No. 95–213, 97 Stat. 1494, December 19, 1977. See Appendix A of this volume.

[10]S. 2567, 96th Cong., 2d. Sess. (1980); H.R. 7010, 96th Cong., 2d. Sess. (1980).

[11]H.R. 7010, 96th Cong., 2d. Sess. (1980).

ing, and utility industries with annual sales or assets of more than $250 million or more than five thousand employees.

The bill would have required such corporations to have a majority of independent directors, and it defined what constitued a nonindependent director: officers and certain former officers and attorneys, investment and commercial bankers, and suppliers and customers of the company having specified relationships with the company. The bill specified the standards of the duties of loyalty and care traditionally imposed on directors, which would be enforceable in federal court by the SEC and by private litigants.

The bill specified that each subject corporation would have to have at least two committees, one a "supervisory" committee and the other a "public-policy" committee; each would have to have a majority of independent directors.

The supervisory committee would recommend to the full board those to be retained as accountants, lawyers, and auditors; oversee, investigate, and receive complaints from employees and shareholders concerning policies and practices of the corporation (and report on them in the annual report); recommend compensation for officers and directors; and design mechanisms and incentives to ensure that corporate officers complied with corporate policies and relevant law.

The public-policy committee would receive, oversee, and investigate complaints from outside the corporation concerning consumer protection, environmental protection, community relations, and law compliance and recommend to the board positions and activities on public policy and political issues.

Additional provisions would have given shareholders a right to nominate persons to the board and the right to approve a wide range of transactions. The bill would also have enlarged the disclosures required to be made, principally in the areas of consumer protection, environment, employee injuries, and the composition of any chemical products, and would have required elaborate protections for employees and communities adversely affected by the closing of facilities.

The Metzenbaum bill followed the report of a committee appointed by Senator Metzenbaum to advise him with respect to corporate governance matters. The committee advocated that boards have majorities of independent directors and that audit and nominating committees be made up of outside directors; however, it did not recommend legislation to achieve these ends.

This bill, considerably more limited in scope than the Rosenthal bill, included findings that boards had failed to exercise "adequate supervision and independent judgment" and that "the shareholder's voice" had been weakened. This bill would have applied to corporations with five hundred or more shareholders and either more than $100 million of inventories, gross property, plant, and equipment comprising more than 10 percent of total assets, or $100 million in total sales or revenues, or $1 billion in total assets.

Like the Rosenthal bill, the Metzenbaum bill would have established federal duties of care and loyalty for directors and, similarly, required subject corporations to have boards of directors including a majority of independent directors. What caused a director to not be independent was similarly delineated but in a slightly less sweeping manner. The bill would have required subject corporations to have audit and nominating committees consisting only of independent directors.

With some exceptions, the duties of the committees would have paralleled those now customary for such committees. The audit committee would have had general oversight responsibility with respect to the corporation's annual audit and with respect to internal controls. It would have had the power to investigate any matter that came within the scope of its duties and would have had the duty of reviewing all communications with shareholders and the public with respect to financial matters and forecasts.

The nominating committee would have had the responsibility and power to nominate directors (not simply to recommend them to the full board for nomination), but shareholders would also have had the right to nominate persons whose names would have to be included in management's proxy statement. The bill would also have required cumulative voting for directors. It contained none of the socially oriented proposals of the Rosenthal bill.

These bills were not reintroduced in subsequent Congresses.

Among the targets of criticism during corporate Watergate was the accounting profession. It was contended by some that if accountants had been more vigilant in conducting audits, the questionable payments would have been timely detected.

As an outgrowth of these criticisms, Senator Lee Metcalf of Montana, chairman of the Senate Subcommittee on Government Operations, commenced an inquiry in 1976 into the accounting profession, which produced a massive seventeen-hundred-page attack entitled *The Accounting Establishment*.[12] This was followed by several days of hearings at which critics and defenders of the profession had their say at length. No legislative initiatives resulted from this.

During the same year Congressman John Moss, chairman of the House Subcommittee on Oversight, also conducted hearings with respect to the accounting profession, though the asserted thrust was the adequacy of the SEC's oversight of the profession. These hearings eventuated in a bill proposed by Congressman Moss and other representatives that would have radically changed the process by which the accounting profession is governed, vesting greater responsibility in the SEC and a National Association of Securities Dealers–like organization to which auditors would be required to belong and which would be subject to the oversight of the SEC. The bill was never reported out of committee.[13]

Of as great, and perhaps even greater, significance than any of the factors mentioned above has been the increasing recognition in the corporate community and among its advisors of the renewed demands for greater attention to corporate governance and corporate accountability. This can be seen by reviewing the tables of contents of business publications ranging from the *Harvard Business Review* to *Business Week* and *Forbes* from the mid-1970s to the present. These and other periodicals have published numerous articles laying out the issues and the manner in which various groups were responding.

Notable among publications reflecting this increased concern were the *Corporate Directors' Guidebook*, published in 1976 by the American Bar Association Section of Corporation, Banking and Business Law, and *The Role and Composition of the Board of Directors of the Large Publicly Owned Corporation*, published in 1978 by the Business Roundtable.

Both reports stated that the boards of the corporations considered by them should consist of a majority of nonmanagement directors. Their recommendations for committee structure and organization were similar, with some modest differences. The bar committee divided independent directors into two groups, affiliated and non-

---

[12]*The Accounting Establishment*, prepared by the staff of the Subcommittee on Reports, Accounting and Management of the Committee for Government Operations, U.S. Senate, 94th Cong., 2d. Sess., December 1976.

[13]H.R. 13175, 95th Cong., 2d Sess. (1978).

affiliated. The former included attorneys, investment and commercial bankers, and suppliers and customers who had recent or proposed dealings with the company above a certain financial threshold. The committee urged that an audit committee should consist only of independent directors, a majority of whom should be nonaffiliated; the Business Roundtable, having drawn no distinction between affiliated and nonaffiliated independent directors, stated that an audit committee should consist only of nonmanagement directors (presumably those designated as affiliated by the bar group would be considered independent). The bar group suggested that there should be a compensation committee with a composition like that recommended for audit committees; again, the Business Roundtable suggested such a committee should be made up of nonmanagement directors. With respect to the nominating committee, the bar group would constitute it exclusively with nonmanagement, nonaffiliated directors; the Business Roundtable suggests that it should have a majority of nonmanagement directors.

The concern of the corporate community was shown by the response of the New York Stock Exchange to the suggestion of Chairman Roderick M. Hills of the SEC in 1976 that the stock exchange mandate that issuers with securities listed there have an independent audit committee. In the face of considerable resistance from some listed companies, the stock exchange, in 1977, adopted a requirement that issuers of listed securities have audit committees made up solely of "directors independent of management and free from any relationship that, in the opinion of its Board of Directors, would interfere with the exercise of independent judgment as committee members."[14] Former employees were eligible to be on the audit committees "if, in the opinion of the Board of Directors, such person will exercise independent judgment and will materially assist the function of the committee." A majority of the committee had to be directors not formerly employed by the issuer or any of its subsidiaries.

The exchange has interpreted this requirement as also mandating a minimum of two outside directors on the boards of listed companies. From time to time the suggestion has been made that the exchange go further and mandate other corporate governance re-

---

[14]New York Stock Exchange, *Statement of the New York Stock Exchange on Audit Committee Policy*, January 6, 1977, p. 1.

forms, such as outsider-dominated boards and independent compensation and nominating committees.

The American Law Institute is engaged in a major project to define the principles of corporate governance. Among the early recommendations of the reporters of the project were proposals that large publicly held corporations be required to have a majority of independent directors (as defined) and an audit committee constituted entirely of such directors.[15]

As a consequence of strong protest from the business community, particularly from the Business Roundtable, the proposal that a majority of the board of a large publicly held company be independent directors was converted into a suggestion that such was a "good corporate practice," but the suggestion was retained that audit committees consisting entirely of such directors be mandatory.[16]

The momentum created by the corporate Watergate has not subsided, although some of the urgency has left the drive for reform of corporate governance. Chairman Williams's successor, John S. R. Shad, a longtime securities professional, did not continue Williams's sermons to the corporate community about governance and the responsibilities of directors. However, the increased incidence of hostile and negotiated takeovers again put a near-blinding spotlight on boards and committees and compelled perhaps the most intensive review of the law relating to directors that has occurred in this country.

At no other time is the responsibility of directors greater, or the complexity of their task and role more apparent, than when their company is the target of an acquisition offer, whether friendly or hostile. The decisions directors make then are truly "terminal." No other decisions directors make are as exposed to the public; none has a more immediate effect upon the fortunes of shareholders than the decisions directors make during those heated, often frenetic, times. If they endorse an offer that appears to be too low, they may be the subject of suit, as were the directors in *Smith v. Van Gorkom*, discussed in the next chapter. If they take measures to thwart the take-

---

[15]H.R. 13175, 95th Cong., 2d. Sess. (1978).

[16]American Law Institute, *Principles of Corporate Governance and Structure: Restatement and Recommendations*, Tent. Draft No. 1, secs. 3.03, 3.05, and 3.06; Tent. Draft No. 2, secs. 3.04, 3.05, 3.06, and 3.07.

over attempt and keep the company independent, directors may again be the targets of frustrated shareholders, as were the directors of Marshall Field when they turned aside Carter Hawley Hale.[17] In such litigation, the minutiae of directorial conduct are put under the powerful lens of judicial scrutiny, and sometimes very adverse inferences are drawn.

It is at such times that the independent directors come into the limelight. The inside directors are usually suspect. They generally have carved secure careers with the target and have expectations of rounding out their working years with it and then retiring comfortably on the benefits they have earned by their service. When an offer is made for the company, all these expectations are put in jeopardy. Hence, not unreasonably, courts and shareholders alike suspect that in the cauldron of a possible takeover the decisions made by inside directors may be tainted with self-interest. Consequently, courts are particularly interested in whether the independent directors have endorsed actions taken by the corporation in defending, preferring one bidder over another, or acquiescing in an offer, and they are quick to note relationships that may impair the independence of a board member.

As will be discussed more fully in Chapter 9, it has become commonplace for boards to consitute all or some of the outside directors as a committee to review and make recommendations about the corporation's reponse to an offer.

The acquisition spree of the early and mid-1980s spawned an unprecedented outpouring of litigation aimed at directors, and concepts such as "due care" and "the business judgment rule" were analyzed with an intensity never seen before, largely in the Delaware state courts and in the federal courts.

With this explosion of litigation against them, directors became increasingly aware of the protections afforded them against personal liability for fancied or real shortcomings in their conduct. Directors began asking about the limits of the company's directors' and officers' liability insurance, the extent of coverage, and whether it was imperiled. And of course, the same explosion caused consternation in the insurance industry as it confronted defense costs and exposure

---

[17] Panter v. Marshall Field & Co., 646 F.2d 271 (7th Cir. 1981).

to liability vastly beyond anything experienced before. The result was a dramatic increase in the costs of such insurance, a reduction in limits, and often a company's loss of coverage entirely.

All of this, in turn, jeopardized the willingness of outsiders to serve on boards, especially on those of smaller companies, which were often unable to provide any insurance coverage whatsoever.

This led to intensive efforts in the state legislatures, particularly Delaware's, to relieve the apprehensions of directors and to entice candidates into the corporate arena. Thus, in 1986, Delaware adopted amendments to its corporation law that provided that corporations could adopt charter amendments limiting or eliminating monetary liability of directors for alleged breaches of the fiduciary duty of care.[18] Liability because of conflicts of interest, bad faith, and wanton misconduct was left intact.

And once again the collapse of many enterprises, most of them in the financial services industry—collapses often accompanied by or resulting from misconduct on the part of management—generated the puzzled question, Where were the outside directors? And once again at a time when so many forces were deterring responsible people from taking on the burdens of directorship, demands were made for even heightened involvement and responsibility on the part of the independent directors.

Despite these disquieting signs, it is unlikely that outside directors will be relegated to the corporate junk heap. The problem of corporate accountability will remain a vital one in the United States as long as its economy depends upon privately organized and conducted enterprises. But unless means can be found to make the involvement of nonmanagement directors satisfying and challenging without being financially ruinous, other means of accountability will have to be found. In a society already prone to solve its problems through governmental means, it is not likely that inability to rely on independent directors as a key tool in achieving accountability will breed even deeper governmental penetration of the board room. At this time the Rosenthal and Metzenbaum bills may be the patterns of the future.

---

[18]Sec. 102(b)(7), Del. Gen. Corp. L.

SUGGESTED REFERENCES

BROWN, COURTNEY C., *Putting the Corporate Board to Work*. New York: Macmillan, 1976.

The Changing Role of the Corporate Board, A conference sponsored jointly by Northwestern University Graduate School of Management and McKinzie and Company. Evanston, Ill., 1977.

EISENBERG, MELVIN A., *The Structure of the Corporation: A Legal Analysis*. Boston: Little, Brown, 1976.

HEIDRICK and STRUGGLES, *The Changing Board, 1986 Profile of the Board of Directors*. New York: Heidrick and Struggles, New York: 1986.

JURAN, J.M., and J. KEITH LOUDEN, *The Corporate Director*. New York, 1966.

LOUDEN, J. KEITH, *The Director: A Professional's Guide to Effective Board Work*, Chap. 7, "Committees of the Board," New York: AMACOM, 1982.

MAURER, RICHARD S., *Guidelines for Information Flow to Directors*, National Association of Corporate Directors. Monograph. Washington, DC.: National Association of Corporate Directors, March 1980.

NADER, RALPH, MARK GREEN, and JOEL SELIGMAN, *Taming the Giant Corporation*. New York: W. W. Norton, 1976.

The New Director: Changing Views of the Board's Role. New York: Arthur Young, 1981.

The Role and Composition of the Board of Directors of Large Publicly Held Corporation, Statement of the Business Roundtable. New York, 1978.

Staff Report on Corporate Accountability. Securities and Exchange Commission, Washington, D.C., 1980.

WILLIAMS, HAROLD M., "Adequate Information: Prerequisite to an Effective Board." Address by Harold M. Williams, Chairman, Securities and Exchange Commission, before the Financial Executives Research Foundation/American Society of Corporate Secretaries, Philadelphia, Pa., September 16, 1980.

2

THE LAW OF BOARD COMMITTEES

In recent years, as board committees have become widely accepted as an appropriate part of the structure of corporate governance, and a considerable literature concerning them has emerged (particularly about audit committees), the legal dimensions of committees have been little remarked on.[1] Most of the discussion has concerned the duties that might appropriately be assigned to them, the manner in which they should carry out those duties, and the like.

The legal aspects of committees have considerable practical relevance. They may affect the willingness of board members to serve on committees; they may affect the liabilities of noncommittee members for the misfeasance or malfeasance of committee members; and, of course, they affect the liabilities of the committee members themselves. Legal considerations may also be significant in determining the extent to which a board may delegate responsibilities to a committee.

We must look to the general principles of corporate law to determine the legal role, functions, and powers of committees; the power of boards of directors to appoint committees; the standards that govern directors in making such appointments; the extent to which noncommittee directors may rely on actions of the committee and escape liability for its misdeeds; the duties of committee members; the authority the committee may exercise; and the duties that may be delegated to committee members.

GENERAL PRINCIPLES

Much of the law relevant to committees depends upon and derives from the general principles governing the conduct of directors. Without embarking upon an extensive discussion of these principles, it is important to note their principal characteristics.

The first duty owed by a director to a corporation and its shareholders is the duty of care. This duty has been repeatedly articulated by courts and, more recently, in statutes. The Revised Model

[1]See Appendix C for a description of committees of the board.

Business Corporation Act (1984) was adopted by the Corporate Laws Committee of the American Bar Association Section of Corporation, Banking and Business Law and will undoubtedly be the model for many states in revising their corporation laws. It defines the duty of care in the following fashion:

> A director shall discharge his duties as a director, including his duties as a member of a committee:
>
> (1) in good faith;
> (2) with the care an ordinarily prudent person in a like position would exercise under similar circumstances; and
> (3) in a manner he reasonably believes to be in the best interests of the corporation.[2]

The Revised Model Act makes explicit the applicability of this standard to the conduct of a director as a member of a committee. Some state statutes stating the duty of care of directors do not make such a provision, but those statutes have usually been interpreted as providing a standard for directors in carrying out their duties as committee members.

A second duty of directors is the duty of loyalty. This means that a director must not act as a director with respect to a matter in which he or she has a personal interest; for example, a director should not participate in the decision of the board with respect to approval of a contract where he or she is the opposite party. The number of potential conflicts is legion. In general, a director must always act in the interests of the corporation and the shareholders and must never put his or her own interests or the interests of those with whom he or she is closely associated ahead of those of the corporation and shareholders. And, of course, this standard also governs a director's conduct as a member of a committee.

A third basic principle to be borne in mind is the business judgment rule. This is a judge-created doctrine that is intended to protect directors against judicial second-guessing of their judgment. Essentially the rule states that in the absence of fraud, illegality, or bad faith on the part of a director, a court will not fault the director's judgment, even if in hindsight it proves to have been faulty, if the judgment had any rational basis whatsoever. Relying upon

[2]Section 8.30, Revised Model Business Corporation Act (1984). See Appendix D for more information.

the business judgment rule, the courts have accorded to directors a wide latitude in conducting the affairs of the corporation.

In 1985, the Delaware Supreme Court wrote a significant gloss on the business judgment rule in *Smith v. Van Gorkom.*[3] In this case the directors of a Delaware corporation hastily approved a proposed sale of the company at a board meeting on the basis almost exclusively of representations by the chief executive officer, without the benefit of any input from investment bankers, examination of the proposed agreement, or other effort to explore the alternatives that might be available.

The Delaware court determined that the directors had failed to inform themselves concerning the transaction in the manner in which they should have, and hence they were not entitled to the benefits of the business judgment rule.

This decision, not surprisingly, caused alarms to sound in boardrooms throughout the country and undoubtedly had a number of ramifications, not the least of which was the tightening of the directors' and officers' liability insurance market and the efforts in several states, notably Delaware, to provide additional statutory safeguards for directors.

The *Van Gorkom* decision, of course, was in the context of a sale of the company, and in those situations courts are increasingly inclined to examine very closely the conduct of directors; in such a circumstance a court may be expected to view harshly decisions made on the basis of inadequate information. However, it may be expected that in any litigation disputing directors' action courts will be urged to pass judgment on the quality and quantity of information the directors had available when they acted.

POWER OF THE BOARD TO APPOINT COMMITTEES

As late as the early part of this century, there was some doubt whether directors could delegate any of their responsibilities to a committee of the board, although it was accepted from the inception of corporations that directors could delegate functions and responsibilities to officers and other employees. This hesitancy gave way to the notion that boards could delegate some of their functions to committees.

[3]488 A.2d 858 (Del. Superior, 1985).

A distinction was sometimes made between ministerial functions (i.e., the execution of determinations of the board or the performance of routine chores) and discretionary functions (i.e., determinations having legal effect similar to actions of the board itself). Gradually this distinction yielded to the principle, now generally accepted and incorporated in state corporation laws, that boards may delegate portions of their authority to committees that, within the scope of the authority delegated to them, may act as effectively as the board.

Initially, discussion centered on the power of boards to delegate authority to an executive committee (see Chapter 3). This committee was generally perceived as exercising the full power of the board, with certain specified exceptions, between meetings of the board. Once quite common, these committees may be declining in importance, largely because ideas about the proper function of a board has changed. Principally this shift has been from the concept that a board should *manage* its corporation to the idea that a board should *monitor* the management of the corporation.

The statutes authorizing board appointment of committees vary significantly in their details. Several jurisdictions provide only for the appointment of executive committees. Such a limitation on a board's power of appointment raises a host of interesting, and to some extent unanswerable, questions. There is generally no statutory set of duties that constitutes the mandate to an executive committee; generally a board may delegate any of its powers and responsibilities, other than those that are specifically stated to be nondelegable. Hence, it is not inconsistent with such a statute for a board to delegate to an "executive" committee the duties, inter alia, that are typically given to a "specialized" committee, such as an audit committee.

However, if in such states a corporation desires to have not only an executive committee but a specified additional body such as an audit committee, the problems become somewhat more complicated. Clearly the establishment of another committee when the corporation already had an executive committee and the delegation to it of dispositive, substantive powers that it might exercise in lieu of the board's doing so would appear to be inconsistent with such a statute and might raise serious questions concerning the validity of any action taken by such a committee.

Typically, however, committees are not given such dispositive, substantive powers. Usually they do not make decisions that, but for the existence of the committee, the board would make; hence, there would generally be no action taken that might be invalid. The critical question is whether the rules discussed later regarding the ability of non–committee members to rely on the work of the committee would apply in such a situation. It may well be that the non-member directors could rely if they had used appropriate care in the appointment and supervision of the committee.

To the extent that members of board committees may be chargeable with a higher standard of care because of their more intimate involvement in the affairs of the corporation made their peculiar responsibility, one court has indicated that whether appointment of the committee was authorized or not is of no consequence.

The minimum number of directors that must constitute a committee also varies. In twenty-seven jurisdictions, the minimum is two; in six, three; in four, one, and in thirteen there is no specification. The same problems discussed with respect to nonauthorized committees would exist with respect to otherwise lawful committees constituted with fewer than the minimum number of members. The validity of such a committee's acts would be questionable; reliance by a noncommittee director on the nondispositive work of the committee might be permissible if appropriate care had been exercised in selection and supervision.

There are also variations as to the source of authority to appoint committees. In some cases authority must be contained in the articles of incorporation or bylaws with effectuation through board resolution. In others, the board's authority is derived from the corporation statute itself. Thus, a corporation contemplating the appointment of a committee must consult the corporation law of its jurisdiction to determine whether it needs prior authority in the articles or bylaws. Failure to follow required procedures in appointing a committee might affect the validity of its acts and the ability of noncommittee directors to rely on its determinations and work.

Regardless of the source of authority for a committee, appointment is made by resolution of the board. The resolution delineates the authority given to the committee. All statutes that authorize the appointment of committees specify certain activities that cannot be delegated to a committee. Typical of these exceptions are those enumerated in the Revised Model Business Corporation Act:

A committee may not . . .

(1) authorize distributions;

(2) approve or propose to shareholders action that this Act requires be approved by shareholders;

(3) fill vacancies on the board of directors or on any of its committees;

(4) amend articles of incorporation pursuant to section 10.02;

(5) adopt, amend, or repeal bylaws;

(6) approve a plan of merger not requiring shareholder approval;

(7) authorize or approve reacquisition of shares, except according to a formula or method prescribed by the board of directors; or

(8) authorize or approve the issuance or sale or contract for sale of shares, or determine the designation and relative rights, preferences, and limitations of a class or series of shares, except that the board of directors may authorize a committee (or a senior executive officer of the corporation) to do so within limits specifically prescribed by the board of directors.[4]

THE APPOINTMENT OF COMMITTEES

The duty of care applies to all responsibilities of directors. Thus, directors must satisfy the standard of care in appointing committees. The greater the responsibilities accorded a committee, the more care the directors must exercise. It follows that a board must consider carefully the qualifications of members of a committee. Obviously, the choice is limited by the membership of the board and is further limited if a decision is made that the members of the committee should be independent directors. It would appear that the question of whether directors exercised appropriate care in selecting committee members should be judged in terms of the available choices rather than on an abstract basis.

A question arises: If a board includes independent directors, does the duty of care require the appointment of such outside, or independent, directors to a committee? It is difficult to reach the conclusion that it does. Notwithstanding the increasing division of boards between inside and outside directors, all directors are sub-

---

[4]Section 8.25, Revised Model Business Corporation Act (1984). See Appendix D for more information.

ject to the same responsibilities of due care and loyalty to the corporation. Thus, inside directors are expected to perform their duties as committee members in the same manner as are outside directors. Suggesting that a board's duty of care precludes it from appointing insiders to a committee would imply that inside directors were incapable of effectively performing committee duties. That assumption is unwarranted.

However, circumstances may often suggest that certain inside directors should not be appointed to certain committees. For instance, since one of the typical functions of an audit committee is to monitor both the internal and external audit processes and the financial reporting practices of the corporation, prudence would certainly suggest that the corporation's chief financial officer, if a member of the board, should not be a member of the audit committee. It should be noted that the New York Stock Exchange policy with respect to audit committees limits the eligibility of inside directors for appointment to that committee.

Obviously, prudent directors should consider the qualifications of members appointed to a committee. For example, with respect to appointment of audit committee members, directors who appear to have the greatest experience with, and sensitivity to, financial matters of the sort generally within the responsibility of audit committees are appropriate choices. Thus, if a board includes a banker, an investment banker, a retired auditor, or others with similar experience, appointing them to the audit committee would provide additional assurance that the directors exercised due care.

RELIANCE BY NON-COMMITTEE MEMBERS

Members of a board who are not on a committee are concerned about their liability for failures by the committee to perform its duties. To what extent may board members rely on the committee to carry out the functions assigned to it?

Early cases discussed this question in terms of whether the committee was an agent of the board or, in effect, an independent body. If it was an agent, the board would be liable as principal for whatever the committee did or failed to do. If the committee was independent of the board, the liability of noncommittee directors might be somewhat more limited.

That distinction seems to have disappeared, and in its place a judicial and statutory doctrine has emerged that effectively limits the liability of noncommittee directors. Generally, directors not on a committee will not be liable for misconduct by the committee if they exercised reasonable care in appointing members of the committee and if they have exercised reasonable care in monitoring the work of the committee.

The latter would entail, at a minimum, periodic reports from the committee concerning its activities, questioning committee members about any matters not clear in the reports, and general attention to the conduct of the committee commensurate with the importance of the matters being considered by the committee. If members of the board fail to exercise due care in appointing members of the committee or in monitoring the activity of the committee, they may be as liable as committee members for failures of the committee.

Some courts have tied a noncommittee director's ability to rely on committees to knowledge and importance. They have said that if the noncommittee director knew of, or in the exercise of reasonable care should have known of, the transaction questioned, or if the transaction was one of considerable importance to the corporation, then the noncommittee director may have liability. As a further corollary of those propositions, the courts indicate that as the importance of the transaction increases, the greater the likelihood that the noncommittee directors should have had knowledge of it. A few states have provided by statute that noncommittee directors may rely on committees, but these provisions typically provide that directors are not regarded as acting in good faith if they have knowledge concerning the matter that would cause their reliance to be unwarranted.

As a more specific example, Congress enacted the Foreign Corrupt Practices Act (1977), which provides civil and criminal penalties for failure of a publicly held company to maintain an adequate system of internal accounting controls. If a board delegated to a committee, such as an audit committee, responsibilities for overseeing internal accounting controls, due care would suggest appointment to the committee of persons with some experience in internal accounting controls to the extent such are on its board. Further, considering the importance of adequate internal controls in view of the penalties that might be imposed under the Foreign Corrupt Practices Act and the newness of the statutory requirement, it would be necessary for the board to monitor with considerable care the committee's performance, at least during the early period of determining compliance with the statute.

The negative implication of this discussion, of course, is that if the other members of the board fail to exercise due care in appointing members of the committee or in monitoring the activity of the committee, they may be liable for failures of the committee to the same extent as are committee members. Thus, it is of highest importance that the other board members, vis-à-vis the committee, exercise appropriate care as it is defined in the relevant corporation law.

The extent to which directors may rely on committees to perform their duties under the federal securities laws is obscure. The problem is particularly acute under the Securities Act of 1933, which requires that, to escape liability for a material misstatement or omission in a registration statement, a director establish that, after a reasonable investigation, he or she had reasonable grounds to believe and did believe that the statements in the registration statements were true and that there was no material omission.

The extent to which the "reasonable investigation" required by Section 11 of the 1933 Act can be satisfied by delegation to a committee of the board is uncertain. The conference committee report relating to the Securities Act stated that the duty of diligence imposed by the act

> does not, of course, necessitate that he [a fiduciary] shall individually perform every duty imposed upon him. Delegation to others of the performance of acts which it is unreasonable to require that the fiduciary shall personally perform is permissible. Especially is this true where the character of the act involves professional skill or facilities not possessed by the fiduciary himself. In such cases reliance by the fiduciary, if his reliance is reasonable in the light of all the circumstances, is a full discharge of his responsibilities.[5]

One of the few cases to date involving Section 11 and the reliance of directors on others is *Escott v. BarChris Construction Corp.*[6] The case is not instructive with regard to the limits of reliance. The outside directors sought to defend on the grounds that they had relied upon the representations of management and by that means had satis-

[5]H.R. Rep. No. 152, 73rd Cong., 1st Sess. 26 (1933).
[6]283 F. Supp. 643 (S.D.N.Y. 1968).

fied their duty of diligence; not a fatuous argument, since under virtually all state corporation laws directors may rely upon reports of management if they do so in good faith. Two of these directors, newly appointed to the board, indicated that they leafed through the registration statement but had not examined it carefully. While the BarChris analysis is helpful in many respects in fleshing out the cryptic words of the statute, the extent to which reliance may be permissible is still shrouded, but it is clear that blind acceptance of management's representations is unacceptable.

Reliance on a committee to satisfy the due diligence obligation of board members is risky. The language quoted from the conference committee report suggests that reliance may be especially appropriate when "the character of the acts involves professional skill or facilities not possessed by the fiduciary himself." This would appear to contemplate, for instance, reliance on attorneys, accountants, engineers, and others with respect to parts of the registration statement involving matters in which they are expert. Obviously, if the committee contained members with specific skills or knowledge that would be useful in determining the accuracy of the registration statement, a director might rely on the individuals as such, rather than as members of the committee. However, reliance on a committee as a whole to perform the fundamental due diligence investigation required of directors would probably not be defensible. It should also be noted that the liability of directors is singular: The responsibility is the individual director's rather than the board's as a whole. Thus, to rely on a committee to carry out a duty that is imposed on the individual director would appear to be inconsistent with the role of the committee as a surrogate of the board as a whole.

DUTIES OF COMMITTEE MEMBERS

As discussed above, members of a committee are held to the same standard of care in the performance of their duties as directors of the full board. That standard is the care that "an ordinarily prudent person in a like position would exercise under similar circumstances."

There is some suggestion that because of their superior opportunity to be familiar with the matters that lie within their province, members of a committee may be held to a higher standard of care than other directors. A New York court has stated this higher standard.

> Care and skill in management are relative concepts depending not only on the type of corporation, the circumstances involved, but also the corporate role of the Directors. The duty is measured by all circumstances. The fact that the Board delegated certain responsibilities to the defendants . . . as an Executive or Advisory Committee, and they acted as such, is a fact to be considered along with all others present in the case to determine the knowledge they had of the corporation's affairs and possible mismanagement of those affairs. A director is charged with knowledge he actually possessed or which he might have possessed had he diligently pursued his duties. . . . The fact that [the committee] was created and these three defendants served on [the committee] and assumed themselves certain powers and authority by reason of their membership on it is a measure of their responsibility. They are not charged as nonparticipating Directors with acts of mismanagement of their appointees to an Executive Committee. They are charged with their own alleged derelictions. In other words, their duty is measured by what prudent men would do in similar circumstances being in possession not only of the knowledge and information they possessed or could have possessed by diligent attention to all their duties not only as directors and officers, but also as members of the Executive Committee. Having injected themselves into the more detailed management of the corporation and thereby acquired additional knowledge, they are charged with that knowledge in judging their conduct. . . . Their responsibility encompasses matters passed upon by the Committee as Committee members or because of that participation, the diligence required of them was greater and the liability stricter. . . .[7]

Two cases in federal courts tend to confirm this viewpoint. In one the court said:

> What constitutes "reasonable investigation" and a "reasonable ground to believe" will vary with the degree of involvement of the individual, his expertise and his access to the pertinent information and data. What

[7]Syracuse Television, Inc. v. Channel 9 Syracuse, Inc., 51 Misc. 2d 188, 196–7, 273 N.Y.S. 2d 16, 27 (footnotes omitted), summary judgment denied on other grounds, 52 Misc. 2d 246, 275 (N.Y.S. 2d 190 1966).

is reasonable for one director may not be reasonable for another by virtue of their different positions.[8]

Similarly, in the other, the court stated:

The law is that an inside director with intimate knowledge of corporate affairs and of particular transactions is expected to make a more complete investigation and to have more extensive knowledge of the facts supporting the statement than is an outside director, although each must undertake that investigation which a reasonably prudent man in that position would conduct.[9]

In some measure, a theory of liability holding committee members to a higher standard of duty and care recognizes that committees are created to provide opportunities for directors to delegate specialized responsibilities to ease the demands on themselves and to have the capacity for more detailed monitoring of management activities than would be possible without committees. Committee members assume the responsibility for more intensive awareness and care with respect to their particular responsibilities than they had toward such matters before appointment to the committee.

To some extent, both the authority and the duties of members of a committee will depend upon the terms of the resolution (or by-law or charter provision) defining the committee's authority and duties. If it subsequently appeared that a committee failed to perform a duty imposed upon it, and if harm to the corporation or shareholders or creditors could be shown, a prima facie case of liability of members of the committee might well be made. Similarly, if the committee failed to perform a designated duty and the other directors were aware of it or negligently failed to detect the failure, liability might accrue to them too.

Thus, it is imperative that the mandate to the committee be realistic, that it be reasonably achievable, that the committee members periodically review it, and that the board periodically measure the committee's performance against it.

[8]Feit v. Leasco Data Processing Equipment Corporation, 332 F. Supp. 544, 577–78 (E.D.N.Y. 1971).

[9]Goldstein v. Alodex Corporation, 409, F. Supp. 1201, 1203 n.1 (E.D.Pa. 1976).

SUGGESTED REFERENCES

BRODSKY, EDWARD, and M. PATRICIA ADAMSKI, *Law of Corporate Officers and Directors: Rights, Duties and Liability*, chap. 8, "Committees of the Board of Directors." Wilmette, Ill.: Callaghan Co., 1984.

CAPITMAN, WILLIAM G., *Panic in the Boardroom: New Social Realities Shake Old Corporate Structures*. Garden City, N.Y.: Anchor Press, 1973.

CAPLIN, MORTIMER, "Outside Directors and Their Responsibilities: A Program for the Exercise of Due Care," *Journal of Corporation Law*, 1 (Fall 1975) 57.

FEUER, MORTIMER, *Personal Liabilities of Corporate Officers and Directors* (2d ed.), revised by Joseph F. Johnston, Jr. Englewood Cliffs, N.J.: Prentice-Hall, 1974.

GARRETT, RAY, JR.,"What the SEC Expects of Corporate Directors." Address by Ray Garrett, Jr., Chairman, Securities and Exchange Commission, before Arthur D. Little, Inc. Corporate Directors' Conference, December 17, 1974.

KNEPPER, WILLIAM E., *Liability of Corporate Officers and Directors* (3d ed.). Charlottesville, Va.: Allen Smith & Co. Imprinted by Michie Co., 1978.

MATTAR, E.P., and M. BALL, eds., *Handbook for Corporate Directors, Sec. 12—Legal Issues*. New York: McGraw-Hill, 1985.

NASH, JOHN M., *Corporate Directors Guide: Responsibility and Liability under the Current Federal Securities Laws*. Washington, D.C., 1976.

NICOLSON, MIKLOS S., *Duties and Liabilities of Corporate Officers and Directors*. Englewood Cliffs, N.J.: Prentice-Hall, 1972.

Responsibilities of Corporate Officers and Directors Under the Federal Securities Laws. Commerce Clearing House, 1985.

SCHAEFTLER, MICHAEL A., *The Liabilities of Officer: Indemnification and Insurance of Corporate Officers and Directors*. Boston: Little, Brown, 1976.

SOLOMON, LEWIS D., "Restructuring the Corporate Board of Directors: Fond Hopes—Faint Promise?" *Michigan Law Review*, 76 (March 1978) 581–610.

3

EXECUTIVE
COMMITTEES

HISTORICAL DEVELOPMENT

Executive committees are historically the oldest board committees, and while their uses and importance in corporate governance have changed significantly over the years, they are probably still one of the most frequently found, though their incidence is being eclipsed by audit and compensation committees. A 1985 Korn/Ferry study indicated that 79.9 percent of the one thousand largest United States corporations have executive committees.[1] However, the makeup and functions of executive committees have changed immensely over the years.

In times past an executive committee was typically constituted entirely of inside directors and was, in effect, what we would call today a management committee. It would characteristically consist of the top officers of the company, including, perhaps, the heads of the larger divisions. It would meet frequently—weekly or perhaps more often—and virtually all important operating decisions and strategic planning would be reviewed by it. Today most companies have formally or informally established management committees consisting entirely of insiders, generally the key officers of the company. Such management committees, it should be emphasized, are not *board* committees, even though some of the executives who serve on them are members of the board, and even though it may be the practice in some companies to have reports from the management committee as a customary part of directors' meetings.

While executive committees have continued to be a commonplace part of the corporate governance landscape, their prominence on that landscape is significantly less than it once was. This is the consequence of a number of circumstances. First, the jet airplane has made it much easier to convoke directors' meetings, even on very short notice. Where once directors in Los Angeles were two or more days away from a meeting in New York, they can now be on the East Coast for a meeting within a matter of a few hours. More-

[1]Korn/Ferry International, *Board of Directors Twelfth Annual Study* (New York: Korn/Ferry International, 1985), p. 16.

39

ever, coincident with the increased ease of telephone conference hook-ups has been the legalization of telephonic directors' meetings, so meetings of directors can be held upon short notice, and directors in remote parts of the world can be "present" (because of time zones this often entails that directors pull themselves out of bed at odd hours to be able to participate). Furthermore, with the increase of concerns about corporate governance, directors' meetings are held with considerably greater frequency than they once were, with the result that there is not as great a necessity for a body vested with the powers of the board to act in its stead between meetings.

Additionally, increased concern with the effectiveness of boards has resulted in the organization of a number of specialized committees that have in many instances taken over functions that were once performed by executive committees. Audit committees now oversee the internal and external audit function; nominating committees concern themselves with matters relating to composition of the board and often also deal with matters of executive succession; compensation committees deal with executive salaries, bonuses, and other forms of compensation. Previously, many, if not most, of those functions were performed by executive committees.

ADVANTAGES OF EXECUTIVE COMMITTEES

In many companies the executive committee has continued to perform important functions. Telephonic board meetings are not a perfect means of group communication (perhaps televised meeting techniques—much discussed but so far little implemented—will overcome some of the disadvantages). Anyone who has participated in one knows the difficulties: Frequently the transmissions are poor, particularly if some of the participants are taking part with conference-call equipment in one office (someone is always too far away to be heard distinctly). Moreover, the absence of the opportunity to see as well as hear a discussant limits a listener's ability to understand the speaker's reactions and intentions (body language *is* important).

Often an executive committee can thrash out a problem face-to-face and then convoke a full telephonic directors' meeting (or even a face-to-face meeting) to apprise the board of its conclusions and have them ratified.

Executive committees are also important when a course of conduct desirably involving continuing board involvement, such as acquisition negotiations, has been undertaken. Frequently a board will authorize the consummation of a transaction within a range of terms. An executive committee can be of inestimable value to both the board and the officers of a company by monitoring the ongoing negotiation of terms and by being available for consultation with those who have responsibility for the transaction.

Another situation in which an executive committee may be uniquely useful occurs when a board is large and there is the necessity of a number of recurring decisions. Banks, insurance companies, utilities, and other companies with strong community presence will often feel constrained to have large boards. In these situations convening the entire board is burdensome, and sometimes it is difficult to secure quorums. In those circumstances—particularly in institutions such as banks, which have a succession of decisions to make with respect to loans and similar matters—an executive committee that can meet regularly, often weekly, is a virtual necessity.

In many companies executive committees preliminarily screen, discuss, and recommend with respect to matters that are to be brought before the full board. In this role an executive committee enjoys the advantages that derive from working in a small group. The various aspects of a management proposal can be fully discussed, additional information requested, modifications suggested, and alternative courses identified and developed, all of which saves the board as a whole a considerable amount of time. Without such advance work, board action must frequently be postponed because one or more directors wish additional information concerning the matter.

Executive committees are also useful when an emergency arises and management wishes the benefits of authorization from the board in some form, and it is not practicable to convene a telephonic directors' meeting. Many companies maintain executive committees solely for this reason.

Finally, executive committees may be useful if the company is engaged in classified work for the government and a large number of the outside directors do not have the necessary security clearance. Then it is often desirable to constitute an executive committee consisting of those with clearance to exercise the traditional director oversight function with respect to those areas of the company's business.

Because the executive committees were the prototype committees, much of the law relating to committees developed around them. Under all state statutes, boards are given very wide latitude in delegating responsibilities to committees; generally this power is plenary except for those matters specifically reserved in the corporation law or in the charter or bylaws. The only type of committee to which plenary power is typically accorded is the executive committee; as suggested by their names, other committees are limited in function. Thus, except for statutory limits, in many corporations the executive committees' powers are coextensive with the boards', and they can act with the same legal effect unless the boards, in establishing the committees, have put additional restraints on them.

TYPICAL COMMITTEE FUNCTIONS

The functions of an executive committee can be designed in one of several ways. As suggested above, an executive committee can be given authority to act as fully as the board (always subject to statutory limits), including the power to authorize actions that would otherwise be subject to board action: the authorization of capital expenditures and material contracts, the empowering of executives to take certain actions, the approval of bank accounts and signatures on them. Of course, the board can accord an executive committee decisional power but limit it to certain areas or matters.

A second configuration of an executive committee can be to couple the grant of authority to act with a requirement that any action taken be subject to ratification by the full board at its next meeting; of course, the failure of the board to ratify cannot act to deprive third parties of rights they have acquired in good faith as a consequence of action by the executive committee. A requirement of ratification is different from a simple requirement that the executive committee, usually through its chairperson, report actions taken between meetings to the board. Of course, even when the requirement is only to report, the directors can disavow action taken by the executive committee, subject to third party rights.

A third possible means of defining the functions of an executive committee is to deny it any real decision-making power and to confine it to a ministerial role. Under this arrangement the powers of the committee are limited to matters that generally would not come before the board, but which might ordinarily be handled by executives, for example, the supervision of a construction project.

Finally, an executive committee might be confined to simply an advisory function: It would have no decision-making power, but would review proposals to be presented to the board, gather information, and review certain operations. In many companies this is the principal way in which the committee functions, even though the board may not have limited its decision-making power.

Moreso than is the case with other board committees, executive committees typically have a higher proportion of inside directors on it. The Korn/Ferry study indicated that a typical executive committee had six directors, with half of them executives of the company. Given the typical duties of a committee and the desirability of physical proximity to permit quick gathering, this is not surprising (often nonmanagement members of a committee are directors who reside near corporate headquarters).

Reliance upon executive committees, however, is not without its dangers. Mortimer Caplin, a distinguished former commissioner of the Internal Revenue Service and an experienced director, has noted that

> executive committees or their equivalent, with broad overall authority, should be utilized sparingly. Routine matters might well be handled by such committees to save the board's time for more significant problems. But the practice of using an executive committee as a regular clearinghouse—to screen and approve important issues prior to board consideration—tends to downgrade the board and create what has been called "second class" status for non-executive board directors.[2]

The danger identified by Caplin is not confined to executive committees. With the increased ascendancy of audit committees, the same concern has been expressed about them. In some cases boards have tended to load onto audit committees duties that have little relationship to the traditional functions of such committees. For example, an SEC settlement provided that, among other duties, an audit committee would have the obligation of reviewing and approving any settlements that might be made of claims of the issuer against any officer, director, or employee.

The SEC in its Staff Report on Corporate Accountability has

[2]Mortimer Caplin, "Outside Directors and Their Responsibilities: A Program for the Exercise of Due Care," *Journal of Corporation Law*, 1 (Fall 1975), 57, 80.

criticized the sometime concentration of power in executive committees.[3] Reflecting this concern, several of its settlements have included provisions that the companies' executive committees would be restructured in a manner that would better reflect the composition of the board and include more outside directors.

A board majority can, in effect, silence a troublesome minority by using its power to establish an executive committee, elect to it members of the majority, and give it virtually plenary power to make decisions otherwise reserved to the directors, thereby avoiding the contention and questioning that might occur if the issues were brought before the full board.

With the increasing incidence of outside directors, good practice demands that an executive committee, particularly if it is given the power to make decisions rather than simply to advise, should reasonably reflect the composition of the board. Thus, if the board consists of two-thirds outside directors, the executive committee should be similarly constituted. Some departure from this may be appropriate in special situations, for example, if the executive committee is relatively large and its functions are limited to information gathering and advising the full board, a larger proportion of inside directors may be reasonable, provided there are at least enough outside directors on it to constitute a "critical mass."

The above clearly indicates that the creation of an executive committee and its duties depend largely upon the needs of the company, the size of its board, and a number of other variables. However, regardless of the configuration chosen and the responsibilities imposed upon an executive committee, if a company chooses to use such a committee as a part of its governance structure, it should follow certain guidelines.

GUIDELINES FOR ESTABLISHING AN EXECUTIVE COMMITTEE

First, a resolution of a board (or if state law so requires, the articles of incorporation or bylaws) should set forth the duties and powers of its executive committee. If the committee is to have no decision-making power, that should be clearly indicated.

---

[3]Securities and Exchange Commission, Division of Corporation Finance, *Staff Report on Corporate Accountability* (1980), pp. 536–37.

Second, the makeup of the committee should reasonably reflect the composition of the board. If the board consists of twelve directors, nine of whom are unaffiliated with the company, then ideally three-quarters of the executive committee should consist of outside directors. Given the relatively small size of the executive committee, the board should be particularly sensitive to the inclusion on the executive committee of members who, though not executives of the company, nonetheless have affiliations that might be perceived as impairing their independence. Thus, even though outside counsel of the company and the investment banker for the company might for some purposes be considered outside directors, their inclusion on an executive committee without the presence of any other outside director might rob the committee of its capacity to reflect the composition of the board.

Third, the executive committee should report its activities at each meeting of the directors. If its actions are subject to ratification by the directors, then clearly such ratification should occur as promptly as possible, and the directors should be fully informed with respect to all aspects of the action taken, including any third-party rights that might be involved in their action and which might impair the effectiveness of director repudiation of the committee's action.

Fourth, the committee should keep minutes of its meetings, and these should be timely made available to the other members of the board in advance of the directors' meeting. Thus, directors will have a better opportunity to make meaningful inquiries concerning the activities of the committee.

Fifth, the board should carefully consider the constitution of its executive committee. As mentioned, often geographical proximity to corporate headquarters may be a consideration; however, that should not be the predominant consideration. Familiarity with the business, wisdom, judgment, and availability of time to commit to the committee should be of utmost importance. To avoid inordinate closeness between the outside members of the committee and management, the board may wish to consider a rotation policy, for example, a maximum of two or three continuous years on the committee for outside members.

While it may be desirable for directors to serve on committees for more than one year—preferably three to five—so that they can achieve familiarity with the problems within the committees' jurisdictions, companies may wish to rotate members of executive committees more frequently. The "omnibus" nature of a committee's responsibilities does not give a member a continuing and growing familiarity with a particular segment of the board's responsibilities; hence, there is no advantage to continuous membership for a number of years. However, other considerations may militate against frequent rotation. As mentioned, many companies like to have on executive committees board members who live near the company's headquarters. Similarly, if one of the main functions of an executive committee is to provide oversight of defense-sensitive activities of the company by means of directors with clearance, then the universe of directors who may serve on the committee may be so limited that the same members may have to serve for several years.

Executive committees, while not regarded as "working committees" by the ABA Committee *Report on Oversight Committees*[4] and not discussed at all in the Business Roundtable report *The Role and Composition of the Board of Directors of the Large Publicly Owned Corporation*, still have a role in most corporations. Because of the less defined nature of their role, they tend to be overshadowed by the more modern creations—audit, nominating, and compensation committees. While they are less important than they once were, they can be of value in many situations.

SUGGESTED REFERENCES

AURELL, J. K., "The Corporate Executive Committee: A Dilemma For the Non-Member Director," *University of Florida Law Review*, 7 (Spring 1965), 525.

The Business Roundtable, *The Role and Composition of the Board of Directors of the Large Publicly Owned Corporation*. New York, January 1978.

Korn/Ferry International, *Board of Directors Twelfth Annual Study*. New York: Korn/Ferry International, 1985.

MACE, MYLES L., "Management Information Systems for Directors," *Harvard Business Review*, November–December 1975.

MATTAR, E. P., and M. BALL, eds., *Handbook for Corporate Directors*, chap. 15, "Executive Committee." New York: McGraw-Hill, 1985.

Securities and Exchange Commission, Division of Corporation Finance, *Staff Report on Corporate Accountability*. 1980.

---

[4] "The Overview Committees of the Board of Directors," *Business Lawyer*, 35 (1980), 1335.

4

NOMINATING COMMITTEES

HISTORICAL DEVELOPMENT

While the presence of nominating committees as a part of corporate governance structure is newer than that of audit committees (General Motors, which had an audit committee as early as 1939, didn't form a nominating committee until 1972, when, in the words of its former chairman Thomas A. Murphy, it "joined what was at the time only a handful of corporations that had formed such committees"[1]), their importance may in time rival that of audit committees. Roberta Karmel, former commissioner of the SEC, in 1978 said that

> [the nominating] committee can be the single most effective force in improving corporate governance because of its impact over time on the composition of the board and, accordingly, the succession of management.[2]

Evidence of the increasing importance of nominating committees is clearly evident in surveys of board practices. A Heidrick and Struggles report, "The Changing Board,"[3] which is based on a survey of the Fortune 1000 companies in the United States, indicates that in 1986 89 percent of the responding companies had nominating committees, while as recently as 1976 only 9 percent had such committees. Other surveys show comparable growth in their incidence.

IMPORTANCE OF NOMINATING COMMITTEES

The increase in the incidence of nominating committees has clearly been a consequence of the increased attention paid to corporate gov-

[1]Murphy, Thomas, A., "The Nominating Committee: Its Role in Corporate Governance," *Directorship*, 3 (Oct. 1978), 1.

[2]Address by Roberta S. Karmel, "The Nominating Committee as a Corporate Accountability Mechanism," Speech to the Chicago Association of Commerce and Industry, Chicago, Ill., April 28, 1978.

[3]Heidrick and Struggles, *The Changing Board*, 1986 *Profile of the Board of Directors* (New York: Heidrick and Struggles, 1986).

ernance and to the role of directors in strengthening the governance process. The pressure for increasing the number of independent directors was accompanied by concern that even cosmetically independent directors might not be truly independent if they were in effect nominated by the chief executive officers, with the board simply ratifying the choice. Cronyism was seen as a barrier to the accomplishment of the goal of a truly independent body capable of effectively overseeing management.

These qualms were not unwarranted. In many companies the process was indeed (and in some companies still is) one where the chief executive officer was simply and in truth the effective selector of the board: The CEO's nominations were always accepted by the board (after all, *they* held *their* positions because of the largesse and goodwill of the CEO), and in most publicly held companies, absent a proxy contest, those nominated by the board are invariably elected by the shareholders.

The correlative of the nomination process was the process of eliminating directors. Often a director who had become too independent would be politely asked by the CEO to tender his or her resignation. Because the CEO had been responsible for the director's presence on the board, and because there was something of a tacit understanding that the director's service would be at the sufferance of the CEO, invariably a director who had for one reason or another become persona non grata to the CEO gracefully withdrew, usually with some statement of confidence in the company and its leadership and an expression of sorrow that "other commitments" did not permit time to properly carry out directional responsibilities in such a dynamic company.

This process, many vestiges of which still exist on the corporate scene, gave rise to the notion that most boards were puppets of management and could be expected to "rubber stamp" anything proposed by management (ironically, until BP took over the management of Standard Oil Co. of Ohio, the sculpture in front of the new Standard Oil building in Cleveland was slated to be a forty-eight-foot rubber stamp done by Claes Oldenburg).

Nominating committees were perceived by the critics of existing corporate governance procedures as a means of breaking the domination of boards by management. They were embraced by management and boards as a means of enhancing the credibility of boards and, more important, as a means of increasing the effectiveness of boards. Clearly a board that is simply a mirror reflection of a chief executive's style, philosophy, predilections, and beliefs is far less able to make a positive contribution to the corporation than one including a variety of opinions and viewpoints.

While it is impossible to measure the effect of nominating committees on the makeup and effectiveness of boards, the experience of many involved with boards suggests that these effects are affirmative. While the chief executive officer has continued to be a significant influence in the selection of directors, the need for his or her candidates to be acceptable to independent directors has unquestionably affected the characteristics of those whom a CEO suggests as candidates. He or she would be loathe to be seen as trying to "stack" the board with cronies; a committee of independent directors would quickly identify such an effort and refuse to be a part of it.

RESPONSIBILITIES OF NOMINATING COMMITTEES

There is no officially prescribed list of duties of a nominating committee. In 1978 the Securities and Exchange Commission (SEC) proposed that companies subject to its proxy requirements be required to state whether they had audit, nominating, and compensation committees. The commission added that if issuers stated they had such committees, this would "connote that it has committees which perform the functions customarily performed by such committees." The commission then stated that

> with respect to nominating committees, [the functions customarily performed are] selection (or recommendation to the full board) of nominees for election as directors and consideration of the performance of incumbent directors in determining whether to nominate them to stand for re-election.[4]

This effort to define the duties of nominating committees (as well as of the other committees) crumbled under an avalanche of criticism. Instead, the commission required that if an issuer has any of the three committees, it must so disclose and state the duties of each committee. While this has resulted in a good deal of diversity of description, the preeminent duty of a nominating committee is

[4]Securities Exchange Act Release No. 14970 (1978 Transfer Binder, Federal Securities Law Reporter, Commerce Clearing House, Par. 81, 645).

the selection of board candidates to recommend to the board. However, additional chores have been suggested, and in some cases corporations have given nominating committees significant additional duties.

In reviewing possible candidates to fill vacancies on the board, a nominating committee should properly review the needs of the company. While the committee should always insist that candidates be persons of integrity, intelligence, wisdom, judgment, and experience, each company has needs that are more specific. A utility company or a bank holding company may be concerned with the inclusion of directors who have geographical ties with the areas served by the company or its subsidiaries. A company with heavy dependence upon marketing may wish to have on its board one or more persons with unique experience in dealing with marketing problems. A company moving into highly technical fields may wish to change the makeup of its board to include more directors with specialized experience in the fields it is entering.

A nominating committee must be sensitive to the emergence of outstanding talent among minority groups and among women. While it might be true that at one time women and members of minority groups were included on director slates as a response to social pressures and expectations, increasingly it is possible for nominating committees to look beyond race and gender and to select members of such groups less because of that identification than because they can bring significant talent and expertise to the board.

The consideration of board candidates should be a continuous process, not one confined to the time when a director dies or resigns. This means that a committee should be constantly alert to the needs of its company and should maintain an active file of suitable candidates. Senior management members and directors not members of the committee should be encouraged to submit names to the committee.

The SEC proxy rules require that in its proxy statement a company subject to those rules, if it has a nominating committee, state whether the committee will consider nominations from shareholders and if so the procedure shareholders should follow in making such nominations.[5] The overwhelming number of companies state that the nominating committee will entertain shareholder nominations,

---

[5]Item 6(d)(2), Schedule 14A, under the Securities Exchange Act of 1934.

though a few reject such involvement of shareholders. (Anomalously, companies that do not have nominating committees do not have to identify a procedure for shareholder nominations—a strange variant). Generally very few nominations are forthcoming from shareholders, and sadly few of those nominated by shareholders have qualifications that would encourage a committee to give them serious consideration.

At the time a vacancy occurs on the board the activitiy of a committee will quicken, and it will hasten to expand its roster of suitable candidates; however, its chore at those times will be considerably easier if it has continuously identified and considered the qualifications of prospective directors.

In addition to the unique needs of a company, a nominating committee should take into account a number of other factors in considering candidates. One is the matter of time: Will the candidate have the time to be an active board member, including committee commitments? The CEO of a large company who is a member of half a dozen major boards and is active in a number of nonprofit enterprises and activities, notwithstanding the prestige he or she would bring to a board, is nonetheless a bad prospect: Membership on another board would do neither this person nor the company a service.

Another factor to be taken into account is any familial relationship between the candidate and the company or members of its management. While such a relationship is not insuperable, it should be considered, particularly in view of the increasing expectation that boards will be genuinely independent. Thus a sister of the vice-president for finance would generally be a less desirable candidate than someone without such a relationship, but the sister may have unique qualifications that would overcome the negative aspects of her relationship.

Conflicts of interest must be carefully evaluated, especially in light of Section 8 of the Clayton Act. Under this section a person may not serve as a director of two companies if one has an equity in excess of $1 million and if the elimination of the competition between them would be a violation of any provision of the antitrust laws. The Federal Trade Commission has an informal policy of invoking Section 8 when the dollar amount of competition is relatively low. After the recent inflationary surge, this is a small amount; because of this and the diversified nature of many enterprises, a suitable candidate frequently will be barred from becoming a director by the Clayton Act.

Notwithstanding that nominating committees are intended to diminish the influence of CEOs in selecting board members, CEOs must, either as a committee members or otherwise, have a voice in the selection of board members. It is hardly conducive to sound management to force CEOs to accept board members they dislike or in whose competence they do not have faith. However, a sensible nominating committee will be alert to indications that a CEO's objection to a candidate stems less from sound reasons than a concern that the candidate may be truly independent.

Rarely is a nominating committee the final word on board nominations. Typically it makes recommendations to the full board, which has the final authority to approve the nomination for submission to shareholders or, in the case of an existing vacancy, to elect the person.

Critics of the modern corporation sometimes urge that nominating committees, constituted entirely of independent directors, should have the final authority to make nominations. A bill introduced by Senator Howard Metzenbaum in 1980 so provided.[6] This bill also would have established procedures for the placement of candidates on the ballot by shareholders.

The next most important and common duty of nomination committees relates to executive succession, particularly succession to the post of CEO. Frequently this responsibility is given to the compensation committee because its responsibilities often afford it better insight into the performance of executives. In some cases the responsibility is a shared one, with the committees meeting jointly on the matter. In other cases many of the compensation committee members will also be members of the nominating committee, thus bringing to it the insights of the compensation committee. Clearly, if the compensation committee has the responsibility to review the executives of the company for compensation purposes, it is good sense to involve those members in any determinations with respect to the promotion of executives.

Of course, the role of a nominating committee in selecting a successor to a CEO, other than in emergency situations, is usually somewhat attenuated. The most important influence in making that

[6]S. 2567, 96th Cong., 2d Sess. (1980).

determination is usually the incumbent CEO, although in a properly structured corporate environment the final decision is a shared one. In many well-run companies the CEO will prepare and present to the nominating committee (if it is vested with responsibility for recommending a successor CEO) notions of who the successor should be in the event of an emergency and in the normal course of events, as well as the favored successors for other key executives. If the CEO has not taken such action, the committee should urge that it be taken, lest the committee be confronted in an emergency with uncertainty concerning the CEO's opinion. Also, if the committee has the benefit of the CEO's thoughts about those who are qualified to succeed key executives in the company, the committee has time to focus attention on these people and to determine whether they are indeed the logical successors.

In addition to these more obvious duties, increasingly the nominating committee is being accorded broader responsibilities, albeit all related to the constitution and duties of the board.

Many commentators have suggested that nominating committees monitor the performance of incumbent directors to determine whether they should be continued in office, although this function is certainly not widespread at the moment. Courtney Brown, a former dean of the Columbia Graduate School of Business, has observed,

> Methods should be available to the board . . . to deal with incompetence among its members in whatever form it may take, or whenever it may appear in a member's incumbency. This is a delicate matter that may strain mellowed friendships, but it must be dealt with if the work of the board is to be revitalized and if the board is to perform a more significant role. Ways should be devised, in which . . . management need not participate formally, for boards to self-prune their membership when it becomes advisable. The development of an orderly and well-understood procedure to do so within the operating procedures of the board would alleviate some of the hurt feelings involved.[7]

Of course, such an undertaking by the board would entail a notion of what was expected of directors. At the present time only the most egregious misconduct, such as clear signs of intoxication

[7]Courtney C. Brown, *Putting the Corporate Board to Work* (New York: Macmillan, 1976), p. 25.

at board meetings, chronic absence, involvement in a scandal that could reflect on the reputation of the company, is likely to cause a nominating committee to drop a director from a slate or suggest his resignation. Absent such a circumstance, it is probably unrealistic at present to expect a committee to apply a very stringent standard of conduct to incumbent directors. Certainly we are a long way from a time when nominating committees will recommend dropping a director because of age (unless there is an established retirement policy), dozing at meetings, limited competence, inexperience with the matters brought before the board, or anything of the sort. Membership on a board breeds a camaraderie which induces a measure of tolerance of the conduct of fellow board members. However, it is not too much to expect nominating committees to articulate more specific criteria for board membership in connection with future candidates, and perforce some of the incumbents may find themselves wanting by those standards and indicate their unwillingness to stand for reelection.

Many nominating committees have also undertaken to observe and recommend to the board policies concerning the distribution of information to board members. Seeing the company's policies from the perspective of outside directors, they can often identify shortcomings in the company's procedures that would not occur to management. Adequate and timely information is essential if directors are to function effectively. Failure to provide such information is a major failing of management.

In addition to the foregoing functions of the nominating committee, many committees are undertaking to develop policies with respect to the board. These committees review the size of the board and try to determine the optimum size for the board of the company. This may entail an expansion or contraction; the latter is typically done through attrition, by not replacing directors who retire or die. Such committees might also recommend with respect to director retirement policies. Increasingly companies are establishing a mandatory retirement age for directors, usually seventy, and in some cases furnishing limited retirement benefits. While this often deprives a board of able members fully fit to continue performing well as directors, it avoids the problem of dealing with the superannuated director who no longer serves effectively. Also, new members who may contribute more current insights into the affairs of the company can be added to the board without swelling it unduly. Many companies have created the position of "honorary" director to permit retired directors to continue to participate, with the understanding, of course, that they do not have a vote.

Some nominating committees also recommend to the board the committees that should be organized, how they should be constituted, who should serve on them, and what their functions should be. They may also recommend the compensation that should be paid directors, the frequency with which meetings should be held, and where meetings should be held. In addition, some companies expect the nominating committees to monitor developments with respect to boards, observe practices in other companies, and recommend changes that may be desirable for the company.

The size of a nominating committee typically varies from three to five members. Unlike an audit committee, where it is desirable to have members with a fair amount of financial sophistication, there are no particularly unique characteristics that members of a nominating committee should have. However, in keeping with the main purpose of a nominating committee—to assure the independence of the board—the members should desirably be free of any affiliations with the company that might be seen as affecting their judgment. Ideally the company's outside counsel, commerical or investment banker, and persons related to management should not be appointed to the nominating committee.

One of the disputed issues concerning constitution of the committee is whether the CEO should be a member. The American Bar Association Committee on Corporate Laws report on overview committees of the board of directors recommended that a nominating committee should consist entirely of outside directors and that the CEO should not be a member, although it notes that

> a strong view is held by some that, in order to facilitate the fullest participation of the corporation's chief executive officer in the deliberations of the Nominating Committee, he should be a member.[8]

This statement implies that the CEO should in *some* fashion be a participant in the committee's deliberations. The statement of the

[8]The Overview Committees of the Board of Directors," *Business Lawyer*, 35 (1980), 1335, 1342.

Business Roundtable, *The Role and Composition of the Board of Directors of the Large Publicly Owned Corporation,* recommends that a majority of the members be independent but makes no statement with regard to the CEO's being a member of the committee.

Even in companies where the CEO is not a member of the nominating committee, it is not uncommon for the CEO to meet with the committee, particularly when it is considering possible successors for corporate officers and when recommending someone for election or nomination to the board, so that the committee may have the benefits of the CEO's reactions to proposed candidates.

Whichever is the better course for the CEO—membership on the committee or not—in practice the CEO is invariably a part of the final decision-making process in recommending individuals to the full board. Cosmetically there is an advantage in having only outside directors on the board; however, this should not obscure the reality.

Nominating committees, indeed, may be the key to the future governance of United States corporations. Through them corporations may be able to provide greater assurance that the ultimate responsibility of the corporation to its shareholders and to the public is in the hands of persons not beholden to management. Such reassurance could go far to protect corporations from greater interference in their affairs by the government.

A number of recent judicial decisions have suggested to some that courts may be raising the standards of care for directors and may be undermining the protections afforded by the business judgment rule. Moreover, as a consequence of the proliferation of lawsuits against directors, director and officer liability insurance is becoming more difficult to secure; when it is available, it is subject to higher deductibles and lower limit provisions and is becoming much more expensive. In the estimation of many commentators, all this will inevitably result in reluctance to serve as directors on the parts of suitable candidates. As a result, the chore of nominating committees will inevitably become more important and more difficult: Eligible and desirable candidates will be harder to secure, and it will take a goodly measure of persuasion to get them to serve.

As a further consequence of these trends, nominating committees may want to become more involved with management in reviewing director and officer insurance needs and the means of satisfying them.

SUGGESTED REFERENCES

CALDWELL, DONALD R., and L. PARKER HARRELL, "The Nominating Committee: An Emerging Force in the Boardroom," Federal Home Loan Bank Board Journal, 14 (May 1981), 20–23.

CATHCART, SILAS S., "The New Power of the Nominating Committee," *Tempo,* 26 no. 2, 49–50.

"Corporate Directors Guidebook," *The Business Lawyer* 32 (1976) 1841.

HARMAN, J. ROBERT, "The Chief Executive Officer and the Nominating Committee," *Directors' Monthly* (April, 1981).

KORN, LESTER B., *Director Selection Considerations,* National Association of Corporate Directors Monograph. Washington, D.C.: National Association of Corporate Directors, May 1979.

Korn/Ferry International, *Board of Directors Twelfth Annual Study,* New York, 1985.

LOHNES, JACK, "Selecting Directors: The Net Must Now Spread Wide," *Directorship* (November 1980).

MACE, MYLES L., "Management Information Systems for Directors," *Harvard Business Review* (November–December, 1975).

MATTAR, E.P. and M. BALL, eds., *Handbook for Corporate Directors,* chap. 19, "The Personnel, Management Development, and Succession Committee" (New York: McGraw-Hill, 1985).

MUELLER, ROBERT K., "Are Directors Boardworthy?—A Report Card for Board Members," *Management Review* (September 1976) p. 14.

_____, "Criteria for the Appraisal of Directors," *Harvard Business Review* (May-June 1979).

MURPHY THOMAS A., "GM Nominating Committee: Its Role in Corporate Governance," *Directorship* (October–November 1978).

PENNMAN, ALLEN S., WILLIAM T. MEYER, and THOMAS J. SAPORRITO, "A Board's Responsibility for Succession, *Directors' Monthly* (October 1983).

The Role and Composition of the Board of Directors of a Large Publicly Owned Corporation, Statement of the Business Roundtable. New York, 1978.

Securities and Exchange Commission, *Staff Report on Corporate Accountability.* Washington, D.C., 1980.

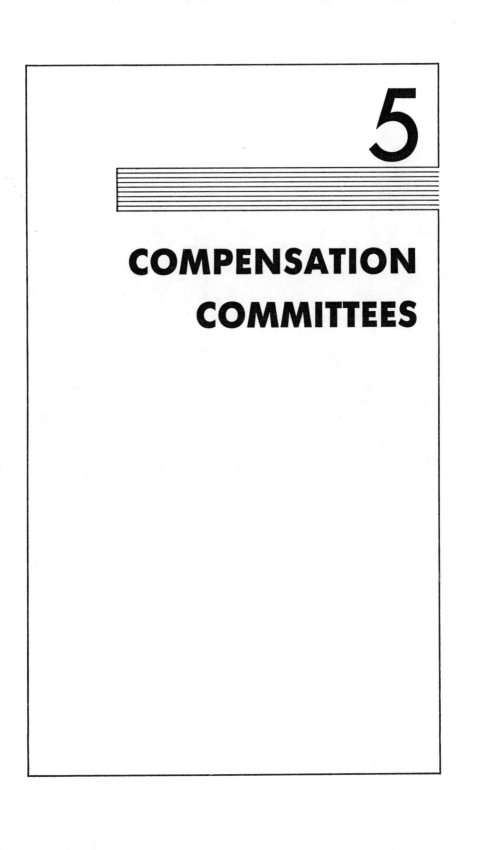

5

COMPENSATION
COMMITTEES

HISTORICAL DEVELOPMENT

The development of compensation committees has received active support from the corporate community because boards of directors recognize the value of this type of committee as a control mechanism. In addition, the Securities and Exchange Commission (SEC) has amended its proxy rules to require a registrant to disclose the existence and functions of audit, compensation, and nominating committees of the board of directors if the registrant had these committees. This undoubtedly caused many boards of directors to establish such committees constituted with outside directors to provide an independent review of management's performance. Indicative of this, the SEC found in a survey of 1,200 companies with compensation committees, an increase to 72 percent from 63.5 percent between 1979 and 1981.[1] This sample included New York Stock Exchange, American Stock Exchange, and over-the-counter companies. Furthermore, a 1985 survey by Korn/Ferry International revealed that 85.5 percent of 633 out of 1,000 of the largest United States corporations had compensation committees. Their survey found that the compensation committees were composed of outside directors who provide for an overall objective assessment of the company's executive compensation programs.[2] Other organizations, such as the Business Roundtable and the American Bar Association Committee on Corporate Laws have actively supported the establishment of compensation comittees. A broad profile of compensation committees is shown in Table 5–1.

BENEFITS OF COMPENSATION COMMITTEES

An effective compensation committee can give assurance to the full board of directors that the officers of the company are appropriate-

[1]Securities and Exchange Commission, "Analysis of Results of 1981 Proxy Statement Disclosure Monitoring Program," Title 17 *Code of Federal Regulations*, sec. 241 (March 1982), p. 35.

[2]Korn/Ferry International, *Board of Directors, Twelfth Annual Study* (New York: Korn/Ferry International, 1985), p. 16.

TABLE 5-1   Profile: Compensation Committees (Sample Means)

Companies by Size and Trading Market[a]	Having Committees (%)	Size	Number of Meetings	Employed by Issuer or Affiliate (%)	Having 6(b) Relationship (%)[b]
All Companies	*72.0*	*3.9*	*3.1*	*12.1*	*15.0*
Over $150	81.5	4.3	3.7	9.6	14.2
50–150	79.6	3.7	2.8	14.1	14.1
0– 50	55.6	3.6	2.2	15.8	17.4
NYSE	*90.0*	*4.1*	*3.9*	*7.8*	*12.6*
Over $150	91.9	4.2	4.1	6.8	13.4
50–150	84.6	3.8	3.5	12.0	9.1
0– 50	84.6	3.4	3.0	8.1	13.5
AMEX	*66.7*	*3.6*	*2.2*	*16.6*	*16.1*
Over $150	81.0	3.8	2.1	13.8	20.0
50–150	82.7	3.6	2.4	14.9	13.6
0– 50	54.7	3.7	2.1	18.9	16.8
NASDAQ-OTHER	*63.5*	*3.9*	*2.7*	*14.3*	*16.6*
Over $150	69.7	4.4	3.4	13.2	14.7
50–150	74.2	3.7	2.4	15.3	18.6
0– 50	54.3	3.6	2.1	15.1	18.0

Source: Securities and Exchange Commission, "Analysis of Results of 1981 Proxy Statement Disclosures Monitoring Program," Title 17 *Code of Federal Regulations*, sec. 241 (March 1982), p. 35.   [b]See p. 67 for an explanation of a 6(b) relationship.

[a]Assets expressed in millions of dollars.

ly compensated on the basis of their managerial performance. In addition, the SEC found in a survey of 1,200 registrants that 22.1 percent of the compensation committees review director compensation.[3] Because it is virtually impossible for the full board to be knowledgeable about every facet of executive compensation, a compensation committee can fill this void through its independent review. A compensation committee can and should familiarize itself with the compensation practices of comparable companies and how in the industry the company's practices compare. The committee's review enables it to identify and analyze executive compensation problems and to make recommendations to the full board of directors. Moreover, its review assists the full board in establishing company policies and discharging its overall responsibility for the company's executive compensation practices.

The compensation committee also enhances the credibility of the executive compensation proposals of the chief executive officer because of the committee's independent and objective analysis and review. The major objective of the committee is to gain assurance that such proposals regarding compensation levels are satisfactory to attract competent executives. An effective compensation program needs to be monitored by an independent review body because the officers are involved in running the company, and the board is charged with overseeing their performance. Such an approach reminds the full board of directors of its ultimate responsibility to the stockholders.

With respect to some perspectives on the compensation committee, Harold M. Williams, former chairman of the SEC, states:

> Another committee which has an important contribution to make to strengthening accountability is the compensation committee. This committee should be the focal point for issues such as the level of executive compensation, the form in which that compensation is to be paid, the noncash perquisites executives are to receive, and the manner and extent to which compensation should be geared to performance. In that latter regard, the compensation committee has a more subtle role in corporate accountability than is typcially recognized. When compensation turns on short term economic performance, for example,

[3]Securities and Exchange Commission, "Analysis of Results of 1981 Proxy Statement Disclosures Monitoring Program." Title 17 *Code of Federal Regulations*, sec. 241 (March 1982), p. 38. For further details see Table 5–2.

it provides added incentive for executives to perform against that measure, perhaps at the expense of longer term viability or broader issues of social responsibility. Corporate compensation systems need to assure that what is being measured and what is being rewarded conform to what the board actually expects of the corporation and its executives. The compensation committee can be the vehicle for incorporating those expectations into the compensation structure.[4]

In addition, Bryan F. Smith, general director of Texas Instruments, asserts that

> the Compensation Committee also plays an important role in strategic planning. In technology-intensive businesses such as those of TI, creative people are the most valuable asset. One of the most complex problems we face is how to encourage creativity while taking only reasonable financial risks. Successes must be rewarded generously, but failures must not be punished so severely that no one is willing to take a risk.
>
> The Compensation Committee offers valuable assistance in finding the proper balance. The committee insists on good wages, benefits and working conditions, and helps to assure that jobs do not become intellectually sterile. In achieving the goals, the committee is aided by the OST system, which involves employees at all levels of the company in the planning process, develops a working environment conducive to innovation, and avoids policies that might stifle creativity.[5]

CHARACTERISTICS OF A COMPENSATION COMMITTEE'S TASK

Committee Structure

The size of a typical compensation committee is an average of four members. This is evidenced by major survey studies undertaken by the SEC, Korn/Ferry International, and Heidrick and Struggles.

[4]Harold M. Williams, "Corporate Accountability—One Year Later," Address presented at the Sixth Annual Securities Regulation Institute, San Diego, Calif., 1979, pp. 27–28.

See Appendix B for Mr. Williams's views on other standing committees.

[5]Bryan F. Smith, "The Board of Directors in Strategic Planning," *Touche Ross Boardroom Perspectives* (New York: Touche Ross & Co., 1981), p. 3.

The SEC found in their study that about 15 percent of the members of compensation committees had a 6(b) relationship.[6] Moreover, Heidrick and Struggles found that compensation committees consisted entirely of outside directors (either independent only or independent and affiliated nonmanagement) in 70 percent of the firms.[7] Korn/Ferry International reports that compensation committees included an average of four outside directors.[8]

Appointments to compensation committees include board members who are chief executive officers, chief operating officers, chief financial officers, or retired corporate executives. Undoubtedly, a knowledge of executive compensation programs and practices is essential to the committee; it is also essential that the committee members have a high degree of independence in order to maintain an objective point of view.

The major objective is to have committee members who have the right balance of skills and experience to review executive compensation issues. If the executive compensation programs are highly complex, it may be advisable to engage the services of an outside consultant. (For example, the management advisory services staff of the company's outside auditors usually offers this type of service.)

The term of office for compensation committee members varies from company to company; however, it is reasonable to expect that the members serve at least two years in order to familiarize themselves with the policies and administration of the executive compensation programs. A board may wish to stagger the terms of service to bring fresh perspectives to its compensation committee's review of compensation plans and programs.

[6]Generally, Item 6(b) of Schedule 14A requires disclosure of whether each nominee or director is: (1) a former officer or employee; (2) a relative of an executive officer; (3) an officer, director, employee or 1 percent equity owner of an entity that is a significant creditor, supplier, or customer of the issuer as defined in the item; (4) a member or employee of a law firm retained by the issuer; (5) a director, partner, officer, or employee of an investment banking firm performing services for the issuer other than as a participating underwriter in a syndicate; or (6) a control person of the issuer (other than solely as a director of the issuer).

[7]Heidrick and Struggles, *The Changing Board, 1984 Profile of the Board of Directors* (New York: Heidrick and Struggles, 1984), p. 5.

[8]Korn/Ferry International, *Board of Directors Twelfth Annual Study* (New York, 1985), p. 16.

Committee Meetings

Korn/Ferry International reports that the average number of meetings is four,[9] although a committee may meet more often if deemed necessary. In general, the role of a compensation committee is to meet in executive session to review and discuss the company's overall executive compensation program. For example, General Electric's management development and compensation committee held ten meetings in 1982. Because it is charged with monitoring management resources, structure, succession planning, development and selection process, and the performance of key executives, the committee reviewed and approved changes in GE's management. Furthermore, the committee approved changes in the company's exempt salary structure and executive compensation programs, including stock option plans and the incentive compensation plan.[10] It appears that in general the frequency of committee meetings will continue because of the complicated issues concerning executive compensation programs. The number of compensation committee meetings is determined mostly by the scope of a committee's charge and the complexity of its company's executive compensation programs.

Generally speaking, compensation committee meetings take place prior to the regularly scheduled meetings of the full board of directors. Although the number of full board meetings varies from company to company, a committee's agenda should include a review and discussion of items such as:

- The company's overall plans, policies, and practices for executive compensation (cash and cash equivalent remuneration for executive officers and nonofficer directors).
- The proposed changes in the incentive compensation plans, including stock option plan, stock appreciation rights plan, and performance unit plan.
- The proposed changes to the company's retirement benefit plans.
- Audits of executive compensation and retirement benefits plans and programs.
- The company's policies concerning management perquisites and the audit committee recommendations.

[9]Ibid., p. 16.
[10]General Electric, *1983 Proxy Statement*, p. 16.

Subsequent to the review meeting, the compensation committee will convene to review management's administration of the executive compensation programs and other benefit plans. The chairperson of the compensation committee will ask the chief executive officer to make recommendations regarding executive salary levels, bonuses, profit sharing, and other incentive compensation arrangements. In addition, the committee will review the compensation levels for the chief executive officer and chief operating officer. The functions of the compensation committee are shown in Table 5-2.

Given the limitations of time, compensation committees need assistance from people who are reliable sources. To meet this need, committees often look to individuals who have responsibility for their company's compensation program. For example, some companies have a compensation director who reports functionally to the compensation committee and administratively to a senior management official.

While a chief executive officer or chief operating officer may supply executive compensation information to a compensation committee, the committee may also look to external auditors or outside consultants for assistance. For example, large international accounting firms very often conduct studies relative to executive compensation practices. These particular studies can be very helpful to committees in terms of how a particular company compares with others in its industry. In addition, outside accounting firms can advise committees on the implications of various tax laws and the reporting of matters concerning executive compensation.

AN ILLUSTRATIVE DISCUSSION OF EXECUTIVE COMPENSATION

In 1983, Irving S. Shapiro, former chairman of DuPont Company, was interviewed by *Executive Alert Newsletter*. This interview is presented in Figure 5-1.

The concept of compensation committees has been well received by the corporate community and the SEC. From the stockholders' standpoint, compensation committees oversee a company's compensation programs to make sure that such programs are reasonable. From the executives' standpoint, committees eliminate any self-interest or self-determination in their own salary structure. Although

TABLE 5-2 Compensation Committee Functions (Sample Means)

Companies by Size and Trading Market	Approve or Recommend Compensation for Senior Management (%)	Adopt Compensation Plans in Which Officers May Participate (%)	Administer Stock Option Plans (%)	Review Compensation Policies (%)	Review Director Compensation (%)	Other Function (%)
All Companies[a]	*92.8*	*42.9*	*37.7*	*63.4*	*22.1*	*28.8*
Over $150	92.1	47.9	42.4	67.1	26.8	33.5
50–150	93.9	42.1	37.1	61.0	17.7	27.4
0– 50	93.1	34.6	29.8	59.0	17.6	21.3
NYSE	*93.8*	*50.8*	*51.2*	*68.8*	*25.0*	*33.1*
Over $150	93.8	52.1	53.1	70.6	27.8	33.5
50–150	96.4	52.7	45.5	70.9	20.0	30.9
0– 50	81.8	18.2	45.5	27.3	0.0	36.4
AMEX	*93.8*	*35.7*	*26.8*	*61.6*	*22.3*	*21.4*
Over $150	88.2	52.9	41.2	58.8	41.2	17.6
50–150	93.0	37.2	27.9	48.8	16.3	27.9
0– 50	96.2	28.8	21.2	73.1	21.2	17.3
NASDAQ-OTHER	*91.6*	*39.1*	*30.6*	*59.7*	*19.7*	*27.8*
Over $150	88.9	41.1	26.4	62.8	23.3	35.7
50–150	92.4	36.4	36.4	60.6	16.7	24.2
0– 50	92.8	38.4	32.0	56.0	17.6	21.6

Source: Securities and Exchange Commission, "Analysis of Results of 1981 Proxy Statement Disclosures Monitoring Program," Title 17 *Code of Federal Regulations*, sec. 241 (March 1982), p. 38.
[a]Assets expressed in millions of dollars.

Figure 5-1 Former Dupont Chairman Talks About Executive Compensation

EA: *How do you view the compensation committee?*

IS: The compensation committee has evolved into one of the key committees in major corporations and has developed a degree of expertise about compensation policy. Board chairmen tend to put some of their strongest directors on that committee today, rather than, as in the past, friendly, old gentlemen who could be depended on.

EA: *Who would you put on the compensation committee?*

IS: I would choose a director who has a high level of intelligence, the right business experience and the guts to speak his mind even about unpopular subjects. If a committee member is honest about doing his job, he ought not to roll over and play dead. As a matter of fact, he's doing the CEO a disservice if he does that, because the function of a good director is to provide the CEO with the kind of assistance he needs to avoid problems. It's also terribly important that the people on the compensation committee be prepared to exercise judgment and not just respond to staff recommendations.

EA: *How would you best communicate compensation policies to the public?*

IS: The corporation has to announce publicly what its standards are. When the corporation reports on compensation, whether in print or orally at its annual meetings, it should demonstrate how management's performance measures up to those standards and justifies the numbers that have been arrived at. The CEO's personal compensation in particular is a matter that has to be addressed and then communicated intelligently. There's a pressing need for the public to understand how corporations compensate their top officers. My experience shows that if the public understands, it will be supportive.

I would apply the principle of full disclosure. As long as there's full disclosure, you'll avoid problems with the public.

EA: *Don't the SEC's proxy statement requirements provide enough information on executive compensation?*

IS: Those requirements are simply a minimum. I think a wise management would go much further in terms of disclosure.

EA: *Such as?*

IS: Two points need emphasizing. First, you ought to separate information on compensation for current performance from all other factors. If you simply lump together salary, stock options, deferred compensation and a whole series of other programs, you wind up with a number that is totally meaningless in practical terms. *[Amendments to the SEC's proxy rules since Mr. Shapiro's comments have met some of these concerns.—Ed.]* What I want to know is, what are you paying that person for last year's performance? Second, good management ought to add an explanation that supplements the SEC requirements and clearly states what the compensation system is and how it's being applied. Then the stockholders have an intelligible basis for judging compensation.

EA: *Besides annual or quarterly meetings, where would you suggest communicating this information?*

IS: There are a number of different ways to communicate it. There's a constant stream of publications coming out of most corporations reporting on what's going on in the business. Employees are just as interested in the subject as people on the outside. Also, I would give the press the kind of explanatory material that corporations now give financial analysts, to help them understand the financial side of the house.

EA: *How do you avoid the self-fertilizing effect in pay raises when a company is being competitive with other companies?*

IS: You don't want to avoid it completely. It's obviously relevant to know what the competition is paying, but that's not the only consideration. Equally relevant is what's happening in your own company. How well did the executive really perform? And I'm not sure I would limit the measure of performance to reported earnings. An executive may be doing a terrific job in managing the company in a very bad situation, such as a recession, and there may be reasons to recognize that in dealing with compensation.

EA: *What are some of the different strategies and approaches you might recommend for different segments of a company?*

IS: I don't want to generalize. Each company has to think about it in its own way. Each business unit has to be assessed in a different way. I think there's no difficulty in knowing which parts of the business are running well and which are trouble spots. But what you want to measure and how you want to set goals in advance and then apply them afterwards are subjects that have to be addressed within each company in terms of its own organization. I don't know of any universal truth that is going to apply across the board.

EA: *What about the use of perks as part of executive compensation?*

IS: In the days when we had a 92% maximum tax rate, perks were a technique for easing the burden. In today's world, where the tax rate is much more rational and reasonable, I personally have great difficulty with a lot of perks. I'd prefer to pay people the money and let them do with it what they want, rather than hide the compensation through the use of corporate aircraft, lodges and other such things. In terms of public perception, perks can do a company more harm than the dollars involved.

EA: *When economic conditions require that a company trim its expenses, should executive compensation be part of the trimming?*

IS: I think there's only one acceptable answer. You can't have two standards if you want to retain the loyalty and support of your organization. You can't expect the average worker to take a cut while the management stands firm or takes an increase. Any management that did that would be a candidate for removal. Equality of treatment in an area like this is absolutely essential.

EA: *If a company cuts compensation, doesn't it run the risk of losing valuable people to other companies that might be in a better position financially?*

IS: The answer is yes. General Motors lost a fair number of good people in the downturn of the automotive industry when it simply had to cut everybody back and some people sought their future elsewhere.

EA: *Should those cuts be paid back in the future?*

IS: No, there's nothing to be gained by that. One can always change compensation programs in the future, based on actual performance. So apart from a very special situation, there ought not to be commitments for the future other than that compensation will be commensurate with business activity and performance. If things pick up and you're doing better, then by all means you ought to readjust. ∎

compensation committees' responsibilities are still evolving for some companies, it is clearly evident that such a committee provides valuable information to the full board of directors.

SUGGESTED REFERENCES

American Bar Association, Section of Corporation, Banking and Business Law, Committees on Corporate Laws, *Corporate Director's Guidebook.* 1978.

American Bar Association, Section of Corporation, Banking and Business Law, Committee on Corporate Laws, "The Overview Committees of the Board of Directors," *The Business Lawyer,* 34 (July 1979), 1837–66.

BACON, JEREMY, *Corporate Directorship Practices: Compensation 1975.* New York: The Conference Board and the American Society of Corporate Secretaries, 1975 and 1978.

The Business Roundtable, *The Role and Composition of the Board of Directors of the Large Publicly Owned Corporation.* New York, January 1978.

COOK, FREDERIC W., "The Compensation Director and the Board's Compensation Committee." *Compensation Review,* 13, no. 2 (Second Quarter 1981), 37–41.

COOPERS and LYBRAND, *Executive Alert Newsletter.* New York: Coopers & Lybrand, December 1983.

General Electric, *1983 Proxy Statement.*

GOLDSTEIN, ELLIOTT, *Counselling of the Board of Directors on its Structure, Functions, and Compensation,* Business Law Monograph. Matthew Bender & Co. Albany, N.Y., 1985.

HEIDRICK and STRUGGLES, *The Changing Board, 1984 Profile of the Board of Directors.* New York: Heidrick and Struggles, 1984.

Korn/Ferry International, *Board of Directors Twelfth Annual Study.* New York, 1985.

KRAUS, DAVID, "Executive Pay: Ripe for Reform," *Harvard Business Review,* 58, no. 5 (September/October 1980), 36–48.

LEAR, ROBERT W., "Compensation for Outside Directors," *Harvard Business Review,* 57, no. 6, (November/December 1979), 18–20, 24, 28.

MILLER, ERNEST C., "Board Compensation Committees at Work . . . A Compensation Review Symposium," *Compensation Review,* 10, no. 2 (Second Quarter 1978), 24–33.

MRUK, EDWIN A., and JAMES A. GIARDINA, *Organization & Compensation of Board of Directors.* Morristown, N.J.: Financial Executive Institute, 1983.

PERHAM, JOHN C., "The Men Who Set Your Salary," *Dun's Review*, 109, no. 2 (February 1977), 75–78.

Securities and Exchange Commission, "Analysis of Results of 1981 Proxy Statement Disclosures Monitoring Program," Title 17 *Code of Federal Regulations*, sec. 241, (March 1982).

STEINBRINK, JOHN P., "Corporate Compensation Committees Showing Their Strength," *Journal of Accounting, Auditing & Finance*, 1 (Winter 1978), 159–63.

6

PUBLIC-POLICY COMMITTEES

HISTORICAL DEVELOPMENT

In recent years, there has been an increasing trend toward the establishment of public-policy committees because boards of directors have overall responsibility for the company's social performance. Heidrick and Struggles found in a survey of 520 companies that only 5.5 percent of the boards of directors had such committees in 1976, as opposed to 31.8 percent in 1981.[1] Such a proliferation of public-policy committees is attributable to increased government intervention and societal expectations regarding a company's commitment to social responsibilty and community support. In view of the fact that a company may be faced with several different types of social issues (e.g., environmental issues, employee issues, community involvement), its public-policy committee can be instrumental in overseeing the company's social performance. (In addition, some large industrial companies in the chemical, pharmaceutical, and process industries have formed environmental safety and health or environmental assurance committees that are separate from the public policy committee.) Accordingly, boards of directors, through their public-policy committees, can discharge their obligations to keep abreast of the social issues affecting their companies.

An example of a board's commitment to social responsibility is that of General Motors, as stated in Figure 6–1.[2]

SIGNIFICANCE OF PUBLIC-POLICY COMMITTEES

The creation of a public-policy committee enables outside directors to have reasonable assurance that management's social performance is adequate. As a result of inadequate attention given to social

[1]Heidrick and Struggles, *The Changing Board* (New York: Heidrick and Struggles, 1982) p. 8. Statistics from their 1984 survey were not available.

[2]Some companies, such as General Motors and General Electric have their public-policy committees and other board committees report separately in the annual stockholders' report rather than in the letter or message to stockholders (see Appendix C).

Figure 6-1   1984 General Motors Public Interest Report

1984 GENERAL MOTORS PUBLIC INTEREST REPORT

This Public Interest Report, the 14th successive annual accounting of General Motors' performance in various areas of public interest, discusses the continuing progress being made by GM to improve its competitive position in the global marketplace and to satisfy its customers as never before.

This progress is being made on many fronts: the completion of a manufacturing joint venture with Toyota that will create an estimated 12,000 jobs for American workers; the initiation of Project Saturn which will fundamentally change the way cars are built in this country; the opening of two all-new U.S. assembly plants, with a third to be completed soon; the continuing application of sophisticated technology to manufacturing, processing, and assembly operations to improve product quality; the conversion of an old auto manufacturing and assembly complex into a totally automated and computer-integrated "state of the art" automotive manufacturing facility; and a major reorganization which consolidates GM North American passenger car and body assembly operations into two integrated car groups which will function as self-contained business units.

Despite the progress being made, little will be truly achieved without greater involvement of our employes. To this end, GM is striving to create an entirely new relationship with its employes—to involve them more in the work place decision-making process, improve the quality of their work life, and enhance their ability to perform as a team. GM's Profit Sharing Plans, the first payout of which was made in March 1984, marks a milestone in employe relations and makes the Corporation and its

employes closer partners in the success of the business.

This Report also describes progress in fulfilling our social responsibilities in such areas as equal employment opportunity; programs of support to minority businesses; the retraining of displaced workers; philanthropic activities in educational, cultural, and medical areas which benefit the public at large; and a food donation program, in cooperation with the United Auto Workers, which provided the equivalent of 20 million cans of food to America's needy.

Although the domestic auto industry has made a dramatic comeback, competitive pressures will continue to demand that old counterproductive ways of doing business be abandoned. General Motors has rededicated itself to being a corporation that keeps open the doors of opportunity. We will continue our aggressive product programs and strategies which, combined with continued efforts to maintain superior financial strength and achieve international cost competitiveness, will provide GM with the appropriate resources and flexibility to strengthen its competitive position for the longer term. And competitive strength translates directly into improved long-term job security.

The future holds risks, but also significant opportunities for our employes, stockholders, dealers, suppliers—indeed, all who have a stake in the Corporation's success. We are confident that these opportunities will translate into meeting the ultimate objective—providing quality products that will result in satisfied customers.

[signature: Roger B. Smith]

Chairman

Reprinted from General Motors, *1984 Public Interest Report*, p. 1.

responsibility, directors may face the potential risk of liability for failure to take action in various areas of public interest. Thus, a public-policy committee's review of its company's plans and programs for social responsibility helps the board discharge its responsibility for problem areas that have an adverse effect on the company's social standing (e.g. company's compliance with government regulations dealing with product safety and equal opportunity).

Furthermore, an effective public-policy committee enhances the functions of such departments as public affairs and employee relations by providing an independent review of these departments. Such a review increases management's performance in implementing social responsibility programs. It also enables the department heads who have responsibility for the company's social performance to communicate attention areas to the board through the public-policy committee.

OPERATIONAL ASPECTS OF PUBLIC-POLICY COMMITTEES

Typically, the duties and responsibilities of a public-policy committee are described in either a board resolution or a charter for the committee in which the scope of the committee's responsibilities should be clearly defined to avoid any misunderstanding between the board and the operating management.

Although the size of public-policy committees varies from company to company, Korn/Ferry International found in their survey of 633 companies that the average number of directors on a public-policy committee is five, with one inside director and four outside directors.[3] This particular mix of directors ensures a high degree of objectivity on the part of the committee because a majority of its members are independent of management. Of course, an inside director, usually a senior management officer, can represent the public-affairs area and, as a result, participate in policymaking.

To make an effective contribution to a public-policy committee, committee members should be knowledgeable about the company's overall commitment to social responsibility. Because of the committee's limited time, consideration should be given to how the information is collected and communicated to the committee. For example, the director of public affairs may report on a functional basis to the committee and administratively to an officer who is responsible for public relations. In addition, the committee may wish to consult with outside experts, such as sociologists who will attest to the company's social performance.

Because members serve at the pleasure of the board of directors, there are no definitive rules with respect to each member's term

[3]Korn/Ferry International, *Board of Directors, Twelfth Annual Study* (New York: Korn/Ferry International, 1985), p. 16.

of service; however, each member should serve at least two years to provide continuity.

Committee Meetings

The potential benefits of a company's public-policy committee depend on its overall assessment of management's response to the changing regulatory environment and the needs of the general public. To meet this challenge, the committee must carefully plan and organize its activities. The number of committee meetings held depends on each company's particular social responsibility requirements and the complexity of its social performance process; it is reasonable to expect a committee to meet at least twice a year— more often, if necessary—to consider matters of public policy. Practically speaking, it is desirable for the committee to schedule its meetings with appropriate company officers (e.g., general counsel, governmental relations officer, employee relations officer, and customer relations officer) to coincide with the preparation of their reports to various regulatory agencies (OSHA, EEO, EPA, etc). For example, the first annual meeting would be devoted to an overall review and understanding of the social issues affecting the company and management's proposed programs for dealing with these issues. The second meeting would be held at the completion of each company officer's regulatory report and other reports before they are issued.

The Planning Meeting

As mentioned above, the public-policy committee meets with the various company officers who are responsible for the company's social performance. Such a meeting involves a review of the overall plan and strategy relative to management's commitment to the various areas of social responsibility. This particular review provides the public-policy committee with valuable information such as the following:

- A summary of the company's social responsibility issues and the proposed programs for addressing those issues.
- An understanding of how management sets priorities relative to those issues and what potential problems that might cause the company to be in violation of government regulations.

- The effect of government regulation (OSHA, EEO, EPA, and so forth.) on management's proposed plans.
- The extent to which management plans to publicize the company's social performance (e.g., by corporate annual report or special public interest report).
- Changes in the public-affairs department relative to organization and operations that affect management's compliance with government regulation.
- The extent to which the public-affairs department uses the services of the internal auditors in such areas as charitable contributions.

Given the wide range of activities that come under the umbrella of social responsibility, a public-policy committee must turn to various officers and their departments for an assessment of matters that have a high priority for their company. The committee is in an excellent position to query the officers about improvements that could be made to enhance the image of the company and to minimize potential legal liability. Further, the information obtained from the various officers through their reports and presentations helps the public-policy committee assess management's social performance.

Review and Evaluation Meeting

The second meeting of the public-policy committee should be held before the company's annual report is issued. The committee should meet with the various public-affairs officers and general counsel to review the reports and results of various statistical studies relative to the company's social performance. The *1984 General Motors Public Interest Report* contains a possible agenda for this meeting (Figure 6–2).

To increase the effectiveness of the public-policy committee, it is advisable to have the public-affairs officers make formal presentations to the committee. For example, the government relations officer could present an overview of how the company is complying with OSHA, EEO, EPA, and other regulatory acts that affect the company. The major objective is to provide assurance to the public-policy committee that the necessary legal and social compliance programs are in place. During the second meeting, the committee might ask some of the following questions:

Figure 6-2

TRANSPORTATION SAFETY
GM And The Passive Restraint
The Evolving Passive Restraint Standard
Changed Circumstances Require A New Safety Strategy
Mandatory Belt Usage
Independent Study Needed On Air Bags, Alternatives
Occupant Protection Through "Built-In" Safety
Drunk Driving And Auto Safety

GM'S INTERNATIONAL OPERATIONS
A Growing Worldwide Commitment
GM Operations Outside The United States And Canada
GM's International History
General Motors In South Africa

THE ENVIRONMENT
Controlling Hazardous Waste
The Clean Air Act Reauthorization: Awaiting Congressional Action
Reauthorization Of The Clean Water Act

THE REGULATORY CLIMATE
Fuel Economy Standards
Industrial Policy: A General Motors Viewpoint
The Need For Decontrol Of Natural Gas Prices

CUSTOMER SATISFACTION
Customer Satisfaction Activities
GM/FTC Consent Agreement
Methanol/Gasoline Blends

PEOPLE PROGRAMS
Quality Of Work Life In Progress At GM
Retraining For The Future
Attendance Procedure Program
Cooperative Effort Saves Plant
Rising Medical Costs/Worksite Health Programs

PHILANTHROPIC ACTIVITIES

PROGRAMS FOR MINORITIES AND WOMEN
Equal Employment Opportunity Summary

TAXES GENERATED BY GM ACTIVITIES

From General Motors, *1984 General Motors Public Interest Report*, p. 1.

- What general statements regarding social responsibility will be disclosed in the company's annual report or special reports?
- Are there any industry trends relative to social performance that the board of directors should be aware of? How does the company's social responsibility policies compare with industry practice?
- Were there any changes in the company's social performance during the year? What was the reason or justification for such changes?
- Have the staff and line officials been diligent in identifying problem areas? How were these problem areas resolved in accordance with the company's social policies?
- Is general counsel aware of any illegal acts involving such laws as OSHA, EEO, and EPA that have not been brought to the attention of the board?
- What are the changes in the company's policies and practices in the areas of affirmative action, environmental considerations, community involvement, product safety, occupational safety, labor relations, and corporate donations?

With respect to the above meeting, the public policy-committee may wish to meet in joint or executive session with the various company officers.

The number of social issues facing public policy committees can be extremely diverse; however, as committees mature, they develop methods for grappling with these social problems. Such an approach enables committees to play constructive roles in helping their boards of directors discharge their responsibilities for social responsibility and social performance.

SUGGESTED REFERENCES

ANDREWS, KENNETH R., "Directors' Responsibility for Corporate Strategy," *Harvard Business Review*, 58, no. 6 (November/December 1980), 30–42.

ANDERSON, ROBERT H., "Auditing SRA Systems: New Uses for Old Standards," *CA Magazine*, 114, no. 5 (May 1981), 47–51.

General Motors, *1984 Public Interest Report*.

HEIDRICK and STRUGGLES, *The Changing Board*. New York, 1982 and 1984.

Korn/Ferry International, *Board of Directors Twelfth Annual Study*. New York: Korn/Ferry International, 1985.

PERHAM, JOHN, "A Useful New Tool for Company Boards," *Dun's Review*, 116, no. 4 (October 1980), 100–102.

RUDER, DAVID A., "Current Issues Between Corporations and Shareholders: Private Sector Responses to Proposals for Federal Intervention into Corporate Goverance," *Business Lawyer*, 36 (March 1981), 771–82.

7

FINANCE COMMITTEES

HISTORICAL DEVELOPMENT

While much attention has focused on the proliferation of nominating committees, compensation committees, and audit committees, there has been an increasing trend toward the establishment of finance committees. For example, Heidrick and Struggles found in a survey of 520 companies that 53.7 percent of the boards of directors had finance committees in 1981, whereas 33.5 percent of the boards had such committees in 1976.[1]

Practically speaking, a board of directors relies on its chief financial officer to execute the financial plans and policies of the company. However, as evidenced by the above statistics, many boards have established finance committees to assist them in discharging their responsibility for their companies' financial policies. The establishment of increasing numbers of finance committees has been a result of voluntary corporate action.

A diligent finance committee can make a significant contribution toward improving a company's financial position. Such a committee provides assurance to the full board of directors that the company's short- and long-term financing plans and policies are adequate. Essentially, this committee reviews and oversees the financial needs of the company and the company's relationship with the financial community. As a result, the finance committee recommends needed or desirable changes in the company's financial and investment policies.

The oversight responsibility of a finance committee is described in General Electric Company's 1982 annual report:

> "The Finance Committee, meeting four times, examined the Company's financial position, its foreign investments, and the operations of the General Electric Credit Corporation."[2]

[1]Heidrick and Struggles, *The Changing Board* (New York: Heidrick and Struggles, 1982), p. 8. Their 1984 survey of 393 companies reported 43.8 percent, p. 4.

[2]General Electric Company, *1982 Annual Report*, p. 50.

NEED FOR FINANCE COMMITTEES

The primary reason for forming a finance committee is that from a practical point of view a full board of directors may not be able to consider the financial issues in detail. The full board may consist of twenty to twenty-five members, which makes the full board's review unwieldy. Thus, it is desirable to have a finance committee that can concentrate its attention on the board's overall responsibilities for the financial position of the company. Moreover, with assistance from external auditors and the chief financial officer, the finance committee can identify trends, analyze management's financing and investment problems, and make recommendations to the full board.

The recent surge in the number of bankruptcies has amplified the role and responsibilities of finance committees. Directors can be held liable for civil and criminal actions for misleading financial statements which includes the financial position of the company. To minimize litigation, a finance committee can scrutinize its company's liquidity position, debt/equity position, profitability performance, and other problem areas, such as leveraged buy-outs and so forth. Through the establishment of a financial controls program, a committee can oversee management's commitments of financial resources; for example, the committee may decide to tighten controls over foreign investments by instituting formal approval procedures at the board level. A finance committee can also assess management's performance with respect to such areas as balance-sheet management, working-capital management, and the capital budgeting system.

BASIC COMMITTEE STRUCTURE AND FUNCTIONS

Committee Structure

To establish a finance committee, the board of directors may pass a resolution in accordance with its company's bylaws or amend the corporate bylaws to comply with state law. To provide a working definition of the finance committee's function and scope of activities, it is desirable to have the committee's charge in writing. While the finance committee's duties and responsibilities should be clearly spelled out, the board should allow the committee the flexibility to pursue areas that have important implications for the financial capabilities of the company.

The size of the finance committee depends on such factors as the size of the company, the size of the board of directors, and the complexity of the company's financing and investing activities. A 1973 survey of companies with finance committees reported that the median size was five members.[3] The consensus seems to be that a typical committee consists of four outside directors and the chief executive officer.[4] Such an arrangement allows for a balance of different points of view and ensures a degree of independence because a majority of the committee is represented by outside directors.

The outside directors of a finance committee should be knowledgeable about the company's financing and investing activities. To make meaningful contributions, members should be highly motivated and inquisitive in the execution of their responsibilities. The chairperson of the finance committee should be carefully selected to provide strong leadership and to manage the delicate relationship with management.

Because finance committees operate part-time, its committee members should agree on the resources necessary to effectively accomplish their objectives. To solve this problem, a committee may request staff support from inside the company; for example, the company's director of financial analysis may head the staff and report directly to the committee on a functional basis. Of course, the duties and responsibilities of the internal staff should be spelled out. Alternatively, the commitee may wish to use outside financial consultants for special projects. This particular service may also be provided by the outside auditing firm, or another accounting firm through their management advisory services. It is also advisable to consult with the director of internal auditing because his or her staff has a high degree of knowledge about the company and because this approach is cost effective.

[3]Jeremy Bacon, *Corporate Directorship Practices: Membership and Committees of the Board*, Report No. 588 (New York: The Conference Board, 1973), p. 59.

[4]The 1985 Korn/Ferry survey indicates that the range is between two (inside directors) and four (outside directors).

The term of office for finance committee members ranges from one year to indefinite terms at the pleasure of the board. In determining the tenure period, the board should consider such factors as continuity and the value fresh perspectives. To accomplish this, the board may consider adopting staggered terms.

Committee Meetings

The number of finance committee meetings is dependent upon the scope of the committee's responsibilities and the complexity of the company's financial resources. There should be a correlation between the review objectives and activities of the committee and the frequency of meetings. Of course, the finance committee may schedule a meeting at any time; however, it is desirable that the committee schedule at least two meetings during the year. The first meeting should be devoted to the short- and long-term financial plans for the company. The second meeting should consist of a review and evaluation of the company's financial position. The following discussion of the agendas for the two meetings is not all-inclusive, and additional times may be added.

The Planning Meeting

A financial planning meeting should be held each year to develop an understanding of and familiarity with the chief financial officer's plans and strategies for the company's demand for financial resources. For companies with a December 31 year end, this meeting should be held sometime in the third quarter period and prior to a full board of directors meeting. This practice will enable the finance committee to give the board an up-to-date report on the strategic financial planning process.

The major topics covered at this meeting might include such matters as:

- The proposed short- and long-term financial goals and needs of the company.
- A discussion and review of external and internal factors affecting the financial position of the company. These would include:
  The economic outlook for the company in terms of anticipated economic growth or recession in the next one to three years.

The expected growth or decline in the industry relative to the company's market position.

The proposed master budget, which includes capital expenditures, production, operating expenses, related sources of funds, and bank lines of credit available to finance these expenditures.

A discussion and review of the strategic planning process relative to both domestic and foreign investments. This would include such matters as the financial policies and controls over investments, market expansion programs, hedging against risks of foreign currency fluctuations, and existing property, plant, and equipment maintenance programs.

In addition to exploring these agenda items, the finance committee should be satisfied that there is proper coordination relative to the financing and investing activities of the company. The major objective is to ensure proper communication between senior management officials and to minimize potential conflicts. Furthermore, the committee should ask the chief financial officer to identify potential financial problem areas and potential financial opportunities for the company. To obtain a clear view of the financial planning process, representative questions are shown in Figure 7-1.

Figure 7-1 Representative Questions for the Financial Planning Meeting with the Chief Financial Officer

---

- What steps did you take in formulating the proposed financial plan in terms of tactical and strategic financial planning activities?
- What matters of financial significance do you plan to cover (e.g., future earnings per share, required bank lines of credit, and working capital targets)?
- To what extent do you anticipate favorable leverage for the company (e.g., return-on-investment leverage and financial leverage)?
- To what extent do you anticipate changes and/or diversification in the capital budgeting system and control procedures? What steps and measures do you take in recognizing risk in capital budgets? Can you provide an overview of cost of capital?
- How do you plan to track capital expenditures?
- How are you handling the forecasting for short- and long-term capital spending?
- What have you developed in the way of computer systems applications for financial information gathering and retrieval?

Review and Evaluation of Financial Position

The second meeting of a finance committee should be held after the completion of the annual audit examination, during the first quarter of each fiscal year. Because several of the review objectives of the finance committee are the same as those of the audit committee, there should be a joint meeting to review the drafts of the corporate annual report and proxy materials. This particular phase of the audit committee's review is called the postaudit interview with the external auditors; it provides an excellent opportunity for the finance committee to ask questions of the external auditors. In particular, the committee may ask the external auditors to provide an analysis of the financial position of the company. The committee's effectiveness can be increased by asking the external auditors and the chief financial officer to present an overview of the statement of changes in financial position. This overview would include a discussion of management's decision making relative to operating, financing, and discretionary activities. Moreover, the chief financial officer can present an overview of the system of financial controls involving the use of company funds.

In view of these review objectives, the finance committee should be satisfied that the agenda includes such items as:

- Management's performance with respect to major areas, such as the company's liquidity position, profitability, capital structure (debt/equity), and securities market position.
- A discussion and review of the major risk and return areas and potential problem areas.
- The impact of inflation on the financial statements and management's response in terms of balance-sheet management and profit planning.
- A discussion and review of managing long-term funds and the factors affecting the dividend policies and decisions of the company.
- A discussion of changes in accounting standards and financial disclosure requirements as a result of new Financial Accounting Standards Board (FASB) and Securities and Exchange Commission (SEC) actions.

For example, the finance committee may ask the external auditors to discuss specific FASB pronouncements that affect such areas as pension plans, foreign investments, inflation, extinguishment of debt, mergers and acquisitions, and lease-buy decisions.

If the committee desires more detailed information, the following Statements of Financial Accounting Standards should be consulted:[5]

Nos. 4, 64, 76	Reporting Gains and Losses from Extinguishment of Debt
Nos. 5, 11	Accounting for Contingencies
Nos. 6, 78	Classification of Short-term Obligations Expected to be Refinanced.
Nos. 8, 20 52, 70	Accounting for Translation of Foreign Currency Transactions and Foreign Financial Statements
No. 12	Account for Certain Marketable Securities
Nos. 13, 17, 22, 23, 26, 27, 28, 29	Accounting for Leases
No. 15	Accounting for Debtors and Creditors for Troubled Debt Restructuring
Nos. 33, 82	Financial Reporting and Changing Prices
Nos. 34, 58, 62	Capitalization of Interest Cost
Nos. 87, 88	Pension Plans
No. 38	Accounting for Preacquisition Contingencies of Purchased Enterprises
No. 47	Disclosure of Long-term Obligations
No. 49	Accounting for Product Financing Arrangements

It is evident that the establishment of a finance committee enables the board to deal more effectively at the senior management level with matters affecting the financial position of the company.

---

[5]The committee should also consult the FASB interpretations and/or technical bulletins where appropriate.

Through a review and discussion of the company's financial plans and the chief financial officer's execution of the company's financial policies, the finance committees can provide useful information to the full board to enhance the financial integrity of the company. Moreover, the committee's periodic review of the financial policies strengthens the relationship between management and the financial community.

With respect to a financially oriented director sitting on a finance committee, Russell E. Palmer, a former managing partner of Touche Ross & Co., states:

> At first glance, having a financial background may appear to place excessive burdens on a conscientious director, while increasing his exposure to liability. In reality, a financial orientation can be turned to advantage, for it enables a director to contribute more to the company in his capacity as a director while he also protects himself legally.[6]

SUGGESTED REFERENCES

BACON, JEREMY, *Corporate Directorship Practices: Membership and Committees of the Board*, Report No. 588. New York: The Conference Board, Inc., 1973.

General Electric Company, *1982 Annual Report.*

HEIDRICK and STRUGGLES, *The Changing Board.* New York: Heidrick and Struggles, 1982 and 1984.

Korn/Ferry International, *Board of Directors Twelfth Annual Study.* New York: Korn/Ferry International, 1985.

PALMER, RUSSELL E., "The Financially Oriented Director," *Financial Executive*, 147, no. 5 (May 1980), 42, 44, 46–49.

ROHRER, JULIE, "Is the Pension Committee of the Board Just Window Dressing?" *Institutional Investor*, 12, no. 11 (November 1978), 83–94.

STACY, F. F., "We Are Doing It—Effectively Using Board Committees," *Management Quarterly*, 23, no. 3 (Fall 1982), 1–4.

WILSON, IAN H., "One Company's Experience with Restructuring the Governing Board," *Journal of Contemporary Business*, 8, no. 1, (First Quarter), 71–81.

---

[6]Russell E. Palmer, "The Financially Oriented Director," *Financial Executive*, 147, no. 5 (May 1980), p. 48.

8

AUDIT COMMITTEES

HISTORICAL DEVELOPMENT

During the 1970s, the role of audit committees received a great deal of attention because of the demands for greater corporate accountability and governance. In view of the increasing size of corporations and the separation of ownership and management, shareholders and other constituencies needed more assurance with respect to the integrity of the internal and external auditing processes and the financial reporting process.

While the Securities and Exchange Commission (SEC), the United States Congress, and the accounting profession actively supported the development and establishment of audit committees, the New York Stock Exchange provided the following mandate in mid 1978. Specifically, "each domestic company, with common stock listed on the Exchange . . . establish no later than June 30, 1978 and maintain thereafter an audit committee comprised solely of directors independent of management."[1] In addition, the SEC found in a survey of almost 1,000 corporations that 87 percent of American Stock Exchange corporations and 79 percent of over-the-counter corporations have audit committees.[2] In Canada, several legislative acts have called for the establishment of audit committees. For example, the Ontario Business Corporations Act mandates that a corporation is legally required to submit its financial statements to its audit committee before such statements are submitted to the board of directors (see Appendix E). Although audit committees are not legally required in the United Kingdom and Australia, the boards of directors of publicly held corporations have formed these com-

---

[1]New York Stock Exchange, *Statement of the New York Stock Exchange on Audit Committee Policy* (New York: New York Stock Exchange, January 6, 1977) p. 1.

[2]Securities and Exchange Commission, "Analysis of Results of 1981 Proxy Statement Disclosure Monitoring Program," Title 17 *Code of Federal Regulations*, sec. 241 (March 1982), pp. 7–8.

mittees to meet changing regulatory requirements and financial reporting needs of shareholders and others.[3]

In addition, there were a series of isolated court actions concerning the establishment of audit committees. For example, in the Penn Central case, the SEC emphasized the importance of the role and responsibilities of corporate directors and recommended increased utilization of outside directors. In the Lums, Inc., Mattel, Inc., and Killearn Properties, Inc., cases, courts required the establishment of independent audit committees and through a court order provided a framework for the duties of audit committees. For example, in the Killearn Properties, Inc., case, the SEC outlined an extensive list of duties and responsibilities for the audit committee. The court ordered the committee to review such matters as (1) the independent audit engagement, (2) the internal accounting controls, (3) the internal auditing function, (4) the codes of conduct, (5) all public releases of financial information, and (6) the activities of the officers and directors.

While the increase in the occurrence of audit committees can be traced to the recommendations of the SEC, the United States Congress, and the American Institute of Certified Public Accountants, and to the mandate of the New York Stock Exchange and court actions, it is evident that such committees increase the awareness of the boards of directors in discharging their stewardship accountability to their constituencies. In view of SEC Release No. 34–15570 on the falsification of corporate books, reports, or accounts, the Foreign Corrupt Practices Act, and the oversight responsibility of audit committees, the shareholders are afforded assurance as to the objectivity of both the internal and external audit processes and the credibility of the financial statements.

AUDIT COMMITTEE ORGANIZATION

Committee Formation

Many companies have formed audit committees by passing resolutions of the boards of directors or amending the corporate bylaws. For a clear understanding of an audit committee's role, its

---

[3]For a chronological account of the significant developments that have led to current audit committee practices, see Figure 8–1.

Figure 8-1 Audit Committee Evolution

1940 As a result of the McKesson-Robbins case, the Securities and Exchange Commission (SEC) recommended the establishment of audit committees (Accounting Series Release No. 19). Specifically, the SEC recommended that the shareholders elect the auditors at the annual meetings and a committee of nonofficer directors nominate the auditors. Also, the New York Stock Exchange Board of Governors issued a similar recommendation.

1967 The executive committee of the American Institute of Certified Public Accountants (AICPA) recommended that publicly held corporations establish audit committees to nominate the auditors and discuss the audit. This course of action would not only assist the boards of directors in discharging their fiduciary responsibility but also provide an independent review of management's financial accounting policies.

1972 The SEC issued Accounting Series Release No. 123, "Standing Audit Committees Composed of Outside Directors." The SEC endorsed the establishment of audit committees by publicly held corporations and also stressed the need for auditor independence.

1973 The New York Stock Exchange (NYSE) issued a white paper, "Recommendations and Comments on Financial Reporting to Shareholders and Related Matters," strongly recommending that each listed company form an audit committee. The exchange also suggested that the audit-committee members be identified in the corporate annual reports.

1974 The SEC amended Regulation 14A dealing with the proxy rules. Registrants are required to disclose in their proxy statements the existence of audit committees and the names of the committee members.

1976 Congressman John Moss, chairman of the Subcommittee on Oversight and Investigations of the House Committee on Interstate and Foreign Commerce, and his colleagues recommended that audit committees have a majority of independent directors.

1977 The Metcalf Subcommittee on Reports, Accounting and Management of the Senate Committee on Governmental Affairs stated in their report "Improving the Accountability of Publicly Owned Corporations and Their Auditors" that the accounting profession or the SEC should immediately require that publicly owned corporations establish audit committees composed of outside directors as a condition for being accepted as a client by an independent auditor.

A NYSE audit committee policy statement required each domestic corporation listed on the exchange to establish and maintain an audit committee of outside directors before July 1, 1978.

Congress passed the Foreign Corrupt Practices Act, which requires every publicly held company to keep accurate accounting records and to maintain internal accounting controls. Also, the boards of directors through their audit committees had to grapple with the antibribery section of the act.

(Continued)

Figure 8-1 (continued)

1978 A special AICPA committee held hearings on a proposal that corporations be required to have audit committees as a condition of an audit. The special committee chose not to recommend to implement such a condition, because the committee felt that audit committees are not "necessary either for the maintenance of auditor independence or for performance of an audit in accordance with generally accepted auditing standards."

1979 The AMEX Board recommended that all American Stock Exchange (AMEX)–listed companies have independent audit committees. However, "the Amex stopped short of making the recommendation a condition of continued listing on the exchange because it was against interfering with the internal affairs of corporations."

1980 Senator Howard Metzenbaum introduced a bill, the Protection of Shareholders Rights Act of 1980, which called for certain large companies to establish audit committees consisting solely of outside directors.

In their *Staff Report on Corporate Accountability*, the SEC recommended that

> while the staff does not believe that an audit committee rule is necessary at the present time due to the significant percentage of companies that have established such committees, it will return to the Commission with further recommendations if the trend in establishment of such committees does not continue or if it appears that further guidance with respect to the functions of audit committees is necessary.

---

duties and responsibilities should be clearly defined and documented. Obviously, a board's charge to its audit committee should be defined in specific terms; however, the committee should be allowed to investigate particular matters that affect audit processes and financial accounting reporting. As the accounting and auditing needs of management change, a committee's charge may be expanded with board approval. Such a limitation on the scope of an audit committee's responsibilities not only enables its board to evaluate the committee's performance but also protects the committee members against asserted claims for their inactions that are outside the jurisdiction of the committee. The scope of the audit committee's responsibilities is described by the General Electric Company:

> This Committee is primarily concerned with the effectiveness of the audits of the Company by its internal audit staff and the Company's independent certified public accountants. Its duties include: (1) recommending the selection of independent accountants; (2) reviewing the

scope of the audit to be conducted by them, as well as the results of their audit; (3) reviewing the organization and scope of the Company's internal system of audit and financial controls; (4) appraising the Company's financial reporting activities (including its Proxy Statement and Annual Report) and the accounting standards and principles followed by the Company; and (5) examining other reviews covering compliance by employees with important Company policies. There were four meetings of the Audit Committee during 1982.[4]

Committee Membership

The size of an audit committee varies from company to company; however, the consensus seems to be that three to five members who are outside directors are adequate. Typically, committee members have varied backgrounds and occupations; as a result, they provide a mix of skills and experience. The argument advanced for this type of composition is supported by the fact that boards of directors through audit committees act as representatives for stockholders. Of course, committee membership should include an individual who has a financial accounting and auditing orientation. On the basis of a survey of 2,459 audit committee members, the Conference Board found that 26 percent were chief executives officers, 12 percent were high-level executives, 9 percent were bankers, 9 percent were retired executives, and the balance had varied backgrounds.[5]

The term of service for audit committee members varies because there is no definitive rule regarding members' length of service; however, it is reasonable to expect that a member should remain in office for at least three years to be effective. A three-year term enables members to acquire the proper perspective and related continuity. It may be advisable to provide some rotation of members to obtain new members with different points of view.

COMMITTEE MEETINGS AND AGENDA ITEMS

There is no prescribed number of meetings, because agendas for audit committee meetings will depend upon the size of the corporation and the complexity of the auditing processes and financial report-

[4]General Electric Company, *1983 Annual Proxy Statement*, p. 16.

[5]Jeremy Bacon, *Corporate Directorship Practices: The Audit Committee*, Report No. 766 (New York: The Conference Board, 1979), p. 54.

ing requirements. Typically, an audit committee meets two or three times a year. Meetings should be scheduled to coincide with the annual auditing cycle, which includes a planning phase, a review and evaluation phase, and a follow-up phase. For example, the planning meeting is held prior to commencing the annual audit engagement in order to discuss the overall scope of both the internal and external audit coverage. The review and evaluation meeting is held after the completion of the annual audit. The primary purpose of this meeting is to discuss the results of both the internal and external audit activities. The follow-up meeting is held before the annual stockholders' meeting to discuss management's actions relative to the external auditor's management letter.

The Planning Meeting

Because audit-committee members are outside directors who often have limited time, it is important that their functions be carefully defined in order to maximize their effectiveness. Any additional activities of the committee should be monitored to avoid an overload of responsibility for which members may not have time. It should be remembered that an audit committee has an oversight responsibility and serves in an advisory capacity to its board of directors. Accordingly, an audit committee should reexamine its charge in order to make certain that its role is clearly oversight and not management. Such a reexamination enables the committee to guard against a dilution of its jurisdictional responsibilities.

Typically, the chairperson of an audit committee will ask those individuals who are invited to the meeting for agenda items. The individuals involved are the outside audit engagement partner, the director of internal auditing, the chief financial officer, and any others, such as corporate legal counsel. The agenda should be distributed in advance of the meeting. Major topics for this meeting will usually include the following:

External Auditing Matters
- Recommending the selection or retention of independent auditors
- The proposed scope and activities of the annual audit engagement (a review of the overall audit plan)

- The proposed internal audit program and its relationship to the scope of the external audit examination
- Discussing the effect of changes in accounting principles, auditing standards, and SEC reporting requirements on the scope of the audit
- Discussing improvements in the system of internal accounting control and the effect on the scope of the audit
- The proposed scope of nonaudit services
- The expected date of completion of the audit and estimated audit and nonaudit service fees

Internal Auditing Matters

- The proposed internal audit program and its relationship to the scope of the external audit plan
- The proposed changes in the system of internal accounting controls and administrative controls
- Discussing any changes in internal audit policies and administration of the internal audit department
- The proposed scope of any special projects or investigations

In addition to these agenda items, the audit committee should discuss management's plan to comply with new regulatory requirements, such as SEC disclosure requirements relative to the Form 10-Q quarterly filing and the annual Form 10-K filing. Also, the committee may discuss any proposed special projects, such as industry analyses and forecasts. Finally, the audit committee may wish to review corporate policies concerning corporate perquisites, conflicts of interest, and questionable foreign payments.[6]

Because an audit committee is a part-time operation, it is imperative that all concerned parties be satisfied with the completeness of the agenda. Therefore, the audit committee members will rely on the independent auditor, the internal auditor, and the chief financial officer to identify areas requiring audit attention and the perceived audit risk and degree of materiality relative to external and internal auditing coverage. For example, areas needing special attention might include the frequency of plant audits, amendments

---

[6]An example of a code of business conduct is provided in Appendix F.

to the corporate EDP plan, potential inventory valuation problems, and other matters requiring management judgment. While the audit committee will not be involved in the details of the auditing procedures, it bears the responsibility for reviewing and monitoring the corporation's financial reporting practices.

With respect to nominating or reappointing independent auditors, the audit committee should give consideration to the level and quality of audit services relative to the financial accounting requirements and operations of the corporation. In addition, the committee should consider the nonaudit services requirements, which include tax services and management advisory services. To assist committee members with the selection process, the American Institute of Certified Public Accountants suggest the following questions:

- What has been the company's past experience with the personnel assigned to the audit? Do they convey the impression that they value the company as a client? Do they seem able to work compatibly—but efficiently and independently—with management and the audit committee? Do they demonstrate an understanding of the company's business problems? Do they anticipate problems and advise the company of new accounting, tax, or SEC developments?

- Can the firm supply the professional services the company needs? For example, does the firm have access to individuals skilled in matters affecting the company (such as industry and SEC specialists or specialists in the problems of smaller companies), and are their skills made available to the company? Does the firm have the capability to serve the company efficiently?

- What are the firm's quality control policies, including its training policies? What is the firm's policy on rotation of the personnel assigned to the audit? On acceptance of clients? On recruitment of personnel? On growth?

- Has the firm satisfactorily explained significant variances in actual fees from estimates? Have suggestions been made for management actions that might reduce fees[7]

[7]American Institue of Certified Public Accountants, *Audit Committees, Answers to Typical Questions about Their Organization and Operations* (New York: AICPA, 1978), p. 15.

The Review and Evaluation Meeting

During the review and evaluation meeting, audit committee members must be satisfied that management is properly discharging its responsibilities for annual financial statements. They need assurance that the financial statements have been prepared in accordance with generally accepted accounting principles. In addition, they want reasonable assurance that the system of internal accounting controls is adequate and that management has devised and implemented a program for compliance with the Foreign Corrupt Practices Act. To obtain this assurance, the audit committee reviews the results of the agenda items of the planning meeting.

Given the SEC requirement that a majority of the board of directors must sign the annual Form 10–K report, the committee members who sign the report review the draft in considerable detail with the independent auditor and chief financial officer. The scope of the review includes both audited financial information and unaudited financial data. The directors should have an understanding of any significant financial reporting problems and the nature and extent of the audit adjustments. It should be remembered that the committee is principally concerned with management's compliance with SEC disclosure rules.

Furthermore, the audit committee should discuss with the chief financial officer and director of internal auditing the quality of both the auditing and nonauditing services, the reappointment of the independent auditors, and the fairness of the audit and nonaudit service fees as compared with those of previous years.

With respect to management's responsibility for the integrity and objectivity of the financial information, many companies include a management report in the corporate annual report.[8] Although this particular report is not mandatory, the chief financial officer may suggest that it be included in the annual report to enhance the shareholders' understanding of management's responsibility.[9]

In view of the audit committee's monitoring of the internal auditing function, the director of internal auditing will meet with

[8]See Appendix G.

[9]See *Illustrations of Management Reports on Financial Statements* by the American Institute of Certified Public Accountants for further guidance (New York, 1981).

the committee to discuss not only the results of the internal financial and operational audits but also the coordinated audit effort with the independent auditors. Here, the director of internal auditing may present an executive summary of the activities of the department. In addition, the audit committee should discuss the quality of the internal auditing function in terms of staffing requirements, budget, and professional development.

For example, the internal auditor could present an overview of the system of internal administrative controls and management's compliance with these controls. Such a presentation coupled with the independent auditors' review of the internal accounting controls enables the committee to acquire a better understanding of management's performance in both the financial accounting and operational areas. This information also allows the committee to obtain a perspective of how the control systems affect the scope of the internal financial and operational audits. In the areas where the control systems are weak, the audit committee in consultation with the auditors should give consideration to the costs and benefits of improving the controls.

As part of the monitoring process, the internal auditing executive may suggest an external review of the internal auditing department. According to the Institute of Internal Auditors, a quality-assurance review should be conducted at least once every three years.[10] Such a review will enable the audit committee to advise the board of directors on the capabilities and future needs of the internal auditing department. Because the independent auditors are required to make an assessment of the competence and objectivity of the internal auditors when relying on their work, the audit committee may request that the independent auditors perform the quality-assurance review. It may be argued that the scope of the review should be limited to certain factors dealing with the quality of internal auditing. For example, the review might include such matters as departmental organization, staffing requirements, professional development, quality-control policies, and organizational reporting responsibility. In addition, the director of internal auditing should discuss with the audit committee the guidelines as set forth in the

[10]Institute of Internal Auditors, *Standards for the Professional Practice of Internal Auditing* (Altamonte Springs, Fla.: Institute of Internal Auditors, 1978), p. 500–2.

Standards for the Professional Practice of Internal Auditing. The bottom line is that an effective internal auditing department provides for an effective audit committee.

The Follow-up Meeting

The primary purpose of the follow-up meeting is to focus on management's actions relative to the material weaknesses in the system of internal control as disclosed in the independent auditors' management letter. Similarly, the audit committee focuses its attention on management's actions to improve the weaknesses in the administrative controls and operating procedures as noted in the internal auditors' operational auditing reports. For example, the audit committee might request that both the independent and internal auditors present an overview of their approaches to evaluating the internal accounting and administrative controls. While the independent auditor cannot express a legal opinion concerning management's compliance with the Foreign Corrupt Practices Act, the audit committee can review the independent auditors' management letter with legal counsel.

Because the content of the management letter is frequently used for management advisory services, the audit committee should request an estimate of the nature and extent of such services that the independent auditors will provide. At this meeting, the director of internal auditing should be present to determine the amount of assistance that the internal audit staff will provide.

Because the follow-up meeting occurs before the annual stockholders' meeting, the audit committee may request a list of potential questions and answers that may be asked of the board of directors from the independent auditor, internal auditor, and chief financial officer. On the basis of their knowledge of the auditing processes and the financial reporting process, these people are in an excellent position to assist the audit committee and board of directors at the annual stockholders' meeting. The major objective is to help the board fulfill its stewardship accountability to the shareholders and effectively discharge its responsibility for due diligence.

From this discussion of audit committees, it is clear that the committee affords a high degree of assurance about the quality of auditing services and financial reporting disclosures. Although audit committee members meet on a part-time basis, their effectiveness can be maintained by having a constructive relationship with the internal and external auditors and the senior financial representatives of management. Such a relationship enables committee members and boards of directors to be aware of financial reporting problem areas and their potential impact on the financial position of the corporation. Audit committee members can help the board of directors not only discharge its fiduciary responsibilities but also minimize its exposure to possible legal liability.

SUGGESTED REFERENCES

American Institute of Certified Public Accountants, *Audit Committees: Answers to Typical Questions about Their Organization and Operations.* New York: AICPA, 1978.

AUERBACH, NORMAN E., "ABCs of Audit Committees," *Financial Executive,* 44 (October 1976), 22–33.

BACON, JEREMY, *Corporate Directorship Practices: The Audit Committee,* Report No. 766. New York: The Conference Board, 1979.

BIEGLER, JOHN C., "Rebuilding Public Trust in Business." *Financial Executive,* 45 (June 1977), 28–31.

BRAIOTTA, LOUIS, JR., *The Audit Director's Guide, How to Serve Effectively on the Corporate Audit Committee.* New York: John Wiley & Sons, 1981.

―――, "Audit Committees: An International Survey," *The Corporate Board,* 7 (May/June 1986), 18–23.

―――, "Audit Committees: Making the Audit Director's Report Effective," *Directorship,* 6 (September 1981), 3–4.

―――, "Guiding the Audit Committee: A CFO's Concern," *Financial Executive,* 51 (September 1983), 52–54.

―――, "How Audit Committees Monitor Internal Auditing," *The Internal Auditor,* 39 (April 1982), 27–29.

―――, "Planning the Audit," *The Corporate Director,* 3 (March/April 1982), 13–18.

―――, "Working with the Audit Committee," *Journal of Accountancy,* 154 (July 1982), 48–50.

BROWNSTEIN, HOWARD BROD, "Audit Committees and Lawyer-Auditor Conflicts," *Directors & Boards,* Spring 1976, pp. 49–60.

CHAZEN, CHARLES, and IRA M. LANDIS, "Audit Committees—Why and How," *The CPA Journal,* August 1976, pp. 33–37.

CHOKA, ALLEN D., "New Role of the Audit Committee," *Practical Lawyer*, 23 (September 1, 1977), 53–60.

Commerce Clearing House, Federal Securities Law Reporter, Chicago (1972–73, 1974–75, 1977–78 Transfer binder pars. 78, 931, 94, 504, 96, 256).

COREY, GORDON R., "Some New Comments on the Directors' Audit Committee and the Audit Function," *The Internal Auditor*, 34 (October 1977), 25–30.

FRAM, E. H., "Insider's View of Audit Committees," *Internal Auditor*, 35 (April 1978), 40–46.

FRIED, DOV, and ALLEN SCHIFF, "Are Corporate Audit Committees Meeting Their Objectives?" *Financial Analysts Journal*, 32 (Nov.–Dec. 1976), 46–48.

Institute of Internal Auditors, *Standards for the Professional Practice of Internal Auditing*. Altamonte Springs, Fla: Institute of Internal Auditors, 1978.

KLOCK, DAVID, and CARL J. BELLAS, "Audit Committees: A Loss Prevention Tool for Directors' Liability," *Risk Management*, 25 (April 1978), 68–69.

————, "Directors Liability Committee and the Audit," *California Management Review*, 19 (Winter 1976), 34–43.

LAM, WAI P., "Development and Significance of Corporate Audit Committees," *International Accountant*, 46, no. 3 (1976), 11–15; also *CA Magazine (CA)*, 106 (April 1975), 32–33, 36–40.

LEWIS, RALPH F., "What Should Audit Committees Do?" *Harvard Business Review*, 56 (May–June 1978), 22.

LOVDAL, MICHAEL L., "Making the Audit Committee Work," *Harvard Business Review*, 55, no. 2 (March 1977), 108–14.

MAUTZ, ROBERT K., and FREDERICK L. NEUMANN, *Corporate Audit Committees: Policies and Practices*. New York: Ernst & Ernst, 1978.

New York Stock Exchange, *Statement of the New York Stock Exchange on Audit Committee Policy*. New York, January 1977.

PALMER, RUSSELL E., "Audit Committees—Are They Effective? An Auditor's View," *Journal of Accountancy*, 144 (September 1977), 76–79.

Securities and Exchange Commission, "Analysis of Results of 1981 Proxy Statement Disclosure Monitoring Program," Title 17 *Code of Federal Regulations*, Sec. 241 (March 1982), pp. 7–8.

U.S. Code 15, Foreign Corrupt Practices Act of 1977, 91 Stat. 1494, Sec. 102.

WILLIAMS, HAROLD M., "Audit Committees—The Public Sector's View," *Journal of Accountancy*, 144 (September 1977), 71–74.

9

SPECIAL COMMITTEES

HISTORICAL DEVELOPMENT AND COURT ACTIONS

One of the legacies of the corporate Watergate is the proliferation of "special" committees of the board. These are called by various names, such as "special investigation committee," "special litigation committee," or simply "special committee."

While such committees were not unknown before the 1970s, it was largely as a consequence of the disclosures discussed in Chapter 1 of corporate illegal domestic political contributions and questionable overseas payments that they became, in effect, an accepted part of the corporate culture as well as a tool dealing with a variety of corporate problems.

Special committees emerged as a distinct part of the corporate structure principally in the context of Securities and Exchange Commission (SEC) settlements of cases in which the commission alleged disclosure failures by public companies. When the SEC believes there has been a material misrepresentation or misstatement by an issuer, it may proceed either administratively (i.e., in a proceeding tried before an administrative law judge) or by an action in the United States district court. In the former case, the commission's remedies are confined to an order compelling correction of the faulty filing; until 1984 the SEC could only proceed against issuers, but in 1984 Congress expanded the SEC's powers and now it may name individuals responsible for the fault.

In an action in a district court, the commission may secure an injunction against defendants (including individuals who have wrongfully participated in the corporation's wrong) barring them from further violations of the law, and it may secure "ancillary relief." This means a judicial order requiring some action on the part of the defendants designed to either remedy the wrong committed or forestall a recurrence of it.

While the courts have often been generous in granting the commission ancillary relief, it has not been in litigated cases that the commission has secured relief entailing the organization and use of director committees; rather, it has been in the settling of cases without trial. In settlements there is no need for the commission to prove to the satisfaction of a court that ancillary relief is appropriate or necessary; about all that is necessary is consent of the defendants. With that the case is generally concluded with a "consent order," a judicial order imposing the terms agreed upon and making them judicially enforceable.

During the 1970s the commission's staff used the consent order process imaginatively and extracted from defendants types of relief not previously sought or secured. A company charged with a violation of disclosure requirements was usually willing to dispose of the matter on a consent basis, thus avoiding the expense and embarrassment of a trial that would entail a considerable drain on management's energies and could result in additional disclosures that could be damaging.

In the eyes of many critics of the commission, the customary injunction resulting from its enforcement endeavors was seen as little more than a slap on the wrist: an order simply to do what the law required in any event. To counter such criticism, as well as to fashion more effective means of assuring that violating corporations complied in the future with the law, the commission's staff began insisting upon the inclusion in consent orders of provisions for some sort of intracorporate mechanism to assure that the terms of the order were carried out and to provide some measure of assurance that the violations alleged did not occur in the future. In many instances the relief secured went beyond those limited purposes and made permanent within the corporation practices and structures that had much wider significance and consequence. The measures that the staff demanded of defendants took many forms and were tailored to some extent by the nature of the violations charged, the then-existing governing structure of the corporation, and the staff's perception of the means needed to achieve what it thought should be done.

In some cases settlements provided for permanent changes in corporate structures. These changes took several forms. If an issuer had not had any nonemployee directors, often the staff would insist upon the appointment, typically, of two or three; in rare cases where the company already had a significant number, the staff might insist upon their increase to a majority. While the commission would not insist upon the right to approve those to be elected, typically it did reserve the right to review whether the candidates were indeed independent of management.

In other instances, if the issuer did not have an audit committee, the commission would seek to secure a settlement including a commitment to appoint one comprised of independent directors. (See Chapter 8 for further discussion.)

Ordinarily the commission did not seek to mandate the duties of either the independent directors or the audit committee beyond those related to any investigation required or the implementation of its outcome; however, in some instances it did impose specific duties. Notably, in one case the commission specified that the newly required audit committee should, among other things, review the engagement of the independent auditors, the scope and plan for their review, and the internal audit system and controls; review with the independent auditors a number of matters related to the audit; make inquiries with respect to compliance with the company's code of conduct; and report and make recommendations with respect to the retention of the auditor.[1] The SEC subsequently proposed substantially this list of audit committee duties as a disclosure item for all reporting companies (if an issuer had an audit committee, it would have had to disclose whether its duties included these), but in the face of strong opposition, it required instead that issuers indicate in their proxy statements what the duties of their audit committees were.[2]

In some cases an order secured by the commission required the company to appoint a special counsel or investigator to probe specified areas of the company's conduct. The assignment of such a person was often to continue or conclude the investigation commenced by the commission's staff or to inquire into an area where the staff suspected wrongdoing but had not pursued the matter. Generally, investigations of this sort were intended to resolve a particular problem and did not entail any enduring corporate change unless the special counsel or investigator so recommended, which they often did.

More frequently, the staff required as a condition to settlement some involvement of the company's directors in this process. In such cases the SEC staff required that the independent directors, a committee of independent directors, or newly appointed independent directors take responsibility for the investigation, select counsel, and in general supervise its conduct.

---

[1]SEC v. Killearn Properties, Inc. (1977–78 Transfer Binder, Federal Securities Law Reporter, Commerce Clearing House, par. 96, 256, ND.Fla. 1977).

[2]Item 6, Schedule 14A, under the Securities Exchange Act of 1934.

As a consequence of these "corporate Watergate" events, the use of special board committees has become commonplace. They are now used for a number of purposes. Principal among these purposes are:

1. To review demands made upon the corporation by shareholders to bring suit against an officer, director, employee, or third party to recover on a claim the corporation allegedly has.

2. When a shareholder has commenced a suit on behalf of the corporation (a so-called derivative suit, one brought by a shareholder on behalf of the corporation to enforce a claim the corporation allegedly has), to determine whether it is in the interests of the corporation to pursue the suit.

3. To investigate a charge originating outside the corporation that company personnel engaged in some sort of misconduct—for instance, falsifying books and records or engaging in conduct violating antitrust or other laws.

4. To investigate charges that surface within the company that there has been misconduct by someone associated with it.

5. To review the propriety of transactions between the corporaiton and an officer or director. This includes determining whether an officer or director is entitled under the applicable law and the corporation's articles of incorporation and bylaws to indemnification for expenses he or she may have incurred in connection with litigation, an investigation, or other proceeding.

Regardless of the purpose for which a special committee is appointed, there are certain measures that should be taken to assure its effectiveness.

First, those appointed to the committee should be indisputably independent with respect to the particular matter they are investigating. Often when it has been impossible to form a satisfactorily independent committee from existing board members, those directors have elected additional directors who clearly had nothing to do with the matter being investigated. Notwithstanding that they are elected by directors who may be suspect, the courts have generally recognized their independence and given their findings appropriate credence.

Second, the committee should enlist the assistance of whatever specialized help it determines it needs. This will often entail the employment of counsel. The counsel chosen should not be at the time or have been in the past—at least in the recent past—associated with the company. In some instances companies have employed their regular counsel to conduct internal investigations. When that has been done, the results of the investigation, if they appeared to exonerate the company and its executives, have been seen as tainted, and frequently the investigation failed to achieve its purposes: to clear the air and snuff out suspicions about the conduct of the company. A notable example of this was an investigation undertaken by a major bank of charges it had manipulated currency transfers improperly to avoid taxes and other laws. It engaged its regular counsel, which had been such for many years and of which it was by far the largest client, to conduct the inquiry. The result was to be expected: considerable skepticism about the counsel's conclusion that the bank had not engaged in any serious improprieties.

In some caes it may be desirable for the committee to retain auditors other than those regularly employed by the company to deal with financial matters connected with the investigation. In recent years there have been numerous charges of "cooked books," and the SEC has brought a number of cases alleging financial reporting improprieties. In those cases it is essential that auditors other than the company's regular ones be retained, since often the vigilance and judgment of the regular auditors may be questioned in the course of the investigation.

Third, the committee should do its work thoroughly and carefully; counsel experienced in such matters can be of inestimable help. In many instances much of the work will consist of tedious poring over documents, lengthy interviews of officers, directors, and employees with knowledge of the events involved, and a careful screening of the wheat from the chaff.

Fourth, the committee should take measures to assure the confidentiality of its work and conclusions, if confidentiality is desired. In this it will need to rely upon its counsel to do what must be done to preserve the desired confidentiality.

Fifth, the committee's work should culminate in a carefully prepared and documented report to the board concerning its conclusions and their basis.

LITIGATION COMMITTEES

Under United States corporation law any shareholder has the right to assert on behalf of the corporation a claim he or she believes it has and which it has failed to prosecute itself. The suit the shareholder brings is called a derivative suit.

As a consequence of the complexity of modern corporate affairs, the proliferation of mergers, acquisitions, and contests for control and the increased aggressiveness and resourcefulness of plaintiffs' attorneys, the number of derivative suits has multiplied dramatically in the last several years (one of the collateral results of this is increased concern with the availability and cost of director and officer liability insurance). Thus, much more frequently than in the past, directors are being called upon to make determinations with respect to such litigation: whether to honor a demand that suit be initiated, whether to move to dismiss the case once it is commenced, whether to settle it.

The law requires that before a shareholder commences a derivative suit he or she must first make demand upon the corporation that it bring the suit itself unless it can be established that for some reason such a demand would be futile. The most common basis for an assertion that demand would be futile is that the directors have a personal interest that precludes them from objectively assessing the desirability of the suit being brought.

For refusal of a demand to bring suit to be effective it is essential that the directors who determine to refuse to bring the suit be independent and disinterested. The fact that they may have voted for the questioned transaction or may be named as defendants in the suit is generally insufficient in and of itself to disqualify them from acting disinterestedly. However, if it appears that the directors do not have the requisite independence, then the demand by the shareholder is excused.

When the suit has been brought by the shareholder, the directors are confronted again with the problem of whether the suit should be prosecuted. During the late 1970s and 1980s, the courts have been responsive to the assertion by corporations that the initiation and prosecution of litigation is properly a management function overseen by the board, and hence, the directors should have the right to determine that the litigation does not serve the best interests of the corporation and have it dismissed.

Starting with that premise, the courts have taken two approaches to the problem. The first, the so-called New York approach, is exemplified by *Gall v. Exxon.*[3]

In this case, decided in 1976 by the United States District Court in New York, an Exxon shareholder commenced a derivative action against the directors of Exxon because of alleged breaches of fiduciary duty in making allegedly substantial improper payments in Italy and violations of federal securities laws for failure to disclose such breaches. The Exxon board appointed a committee of three members, all of whom joined the board long after the alleged payments were made. It is noteworthy that some of the directors who participated in appointing the committee had known of the payments.

On the basis of the committee's determination that it was not in the best interests of the corporation that the action be maintained, the court upheld the motion of the company to dismiss the case. It said:

> It is clear that absent allegations of fraud, collusion, self-interest, dishonesty or other misconduct of a breach of trust nature, and absent allegations that the business judgment exercised was grossly unsound, the court should not at the instigation of a single shareholder interfere with the judgment of the corporate officers.[4]

Thus, if it appeared that the committee members were indeed independent, had not been involved in the alleged wrongdoing, made a reasonable investigation, and had come to a conclusion having some reasonable basis, the court would not inquire concerning the quality of that judgment or substitute its judgment for that of the committee—in other words, the conduct of the committee would be governed by the business judgment rule that governs virtually all decisions of management and the board.

This standard became the accepted one in New York and other states. In Delaware, however, after considerable uncertainty, the state supreme court took a somewhat different tack.[5]

As noted earlier, prior to the commencement of a derivative action, a shareholder must either demand that the directors bring

[3]418 F. Supp. 508 (S.D.N.Y. 1976).
[4]Ibid., p. 516.
[5]Zapata Corp. v. Maldonado, 430 A. 2d 779 (Del. 1981).

the action or be able to establish to the court's satisfaction that such a demand would be futile because of the self-interest of the board.

The Delaware Supreme Court distinguished the procedure to be followed in acting upon motions to dismiss based on committee findings in cases where demand was made and refused by the board, and that in cases where it would have been futile for the shareholder to make a demand upon the directors. In the former case, the Delaware court followed the trend of New York and in effect relied upon the business judgment rule—the directors were entitled to the protection of the business judgment rule if in determining that the suit should be dismissed they had no conflict of interest, they had acted with appropriate care in good faith and in what they believed to be the best interests of the corporation, and their action had at least some semblance of rationality.

However, the court struck out in an unprecedentedly new direction with respect to cases where demand upon the directors to bring suit was excused because of the apparent self-interest of the directors. In these cases the court said the lower court *might* (note that the court did not say the lower court *must*), after independent directors acted in a fashion compatible with the business judgment rule and determined the action should be dismissed, then exercise its "own independent business judgment." The court said:

> The second step is intended to thwart instances where corporate actions meet the criteria of step one, but the result does not appear to satisfy its spirit, or where corporate actions would simply prematurely terminate a stockholder grievance deserving of further consideration in the corporation's interest.[6]

Commentators and some courts that have followed the lead of the Delaware Supreme Court have discarded the distinction between demand required and demand excused; when inclined to opt for the second stage review, they have deemed it appropriate in all cases where dismissal is sought on the basis of a committee determination.

The American Law Institute is engaged in a project to clarify and develop the law and practices with respect to corporate governance, including procedures for shareholder litigation. It has tentatively adopted the Delaware approach, without distinguishing demand excused and demand required cases. The project also pro-

[6]Ibid., p. 789.

poses provisions for the appointment of a person not a member of the board or a committee of such persons to make the necessary determination concerning the continuation of an action in lieu of a committee of directors. This means is intended to make possible the sort of determination an independent committee of the board might make if it is impossible to constitute a sufficiently independent committee from among the directors.

In determining whether an action should be discontinued the committee must consider a number of factors. First, what is the likelihood that the corporation could recover against the defendants and what is the likely amount of recovery? What out-of-pocket costs would be involved in securing the recovery? What effect would the prosecution of the action have upon the effectiveness of executives during the pendency of the case? What would be the effect on morale of employees? What would be the effect on the corporation of the publicity attendant upon the litigation—including effect on customers, suppliers, regulators? In any lawsuit there are a multitude of factors that must be taken into account in determining whether the corporation stands to benefit from the maintenance of the suit.

Litigation committees typically recommend discontinuation of litigation, though that is not always so. In the case of the litigation arising out of the failure of the Continental Illinois Bank, the directors' committee recommended the continuation of the litigation against some of the defendants.

The high incidence of recommendation that the action be discontinued has caused some commentators to criticize strongly these procedures. They contend that cronyism, close association between management and directors, feelings of cameraderie, and such make it unlikely that the action of a litigation committee consisting of directors, no matter how independent they may be on paper, would be totally objective. Such misgivings undoubtedly gave rise to the Delaware procedure, which is intended to provide an additional layer of protection to the corporation.

INVESTIGATING COMMITTEES

Committees of directors are often used to investigate charges of misconduct against officers and others associated with a company. These charges may be made by someone outside the corporation, either official (e.g., the SEC) or private (e.g., a contractor charging kickbacks to executives), or information suggesting misconduct may be generated internally (e.g., a discovery during an internal audit).

In these cases it is often easier to determine which directors are untainted, since the charges will rarely embrace all of them. Further, the alleged misconduct will rarely have been authorized by the board, hence its noninvolvement will be clear.

The scope of the investigation will be determined by the nature of the charges. However, it is not uncommon that in the course of investigating a particular charge evidence will be uncovered of other violations of law or company policy, and sometimes the single incident will be ultimately seen as part of a pervasive pattern of misconduct.

Many investigations of alleged wrongdoing in a corporation entail the possibility of one or more violations of federal securities laws, largely failures to provide financial disclosures or falsification of financial statements, and often it is an investigation commenced by the SEC that occasions appointment of a special committee by the corporation. In some instances the SEC staff can be persuaded to delay the continuation of its investigation pending completion of the company's. This may avoid some of the disruption, rumors, and inconvenience that frequently accompany SEC investigations. If the SEC concludes that the investigation was done thoroughly and competently by disinterested directors and counsel, the results of the investigation will often furnish the basis for a settlement with the commission without further investigation by the staff. However, characteristically, in deferring to the company's internal investigations, the staff will give no assurance that at the conclusion of the company's inquiry, or perhaps during it, the staff will not launch a full-scale inquiry of its own.

ACQUISITION COMMITTEES

As takeovers have multiplied, so has the use of committees of independent directors to deal with them. Directors who are also officers of the company are often alleged to lack the objectivity necessary to judge whether a tender offer is in the interests of the shareholders. Often an unnegotiated bid may jeopardize the officers' jobs and careers; while the officers are bound by the duties of loyalty and care discussed earlier (Chapter 2), many observers believe that personal concerns may override those obligations, if only unwittingly.

Hence, when a bid is made for a company, it is commonplace for the directors to either appoint a committee of independent directors or constitute all of the independent directors in effect a committee for the purpose of reviewing the fairness of the bid and the overall ramifications of it. Their consideration may entail review of the impact the takeover would have not only on the shareholders but upon employees, suppliers, customers, communities, and any others with a stake in the corporation (several courts have stated that such concerns are legitimate ones for directors notwithstanding that their fiduciary obligations run only to the shareholders).

Most courts that have considered the matter have concluded that the concurrence by the independent directors or a committee of them in action taken to fend off an unwanted offer is of significance in determining whether the action was properly taken. In *MacAndrews & Forbes Holdings, Inc. v. Revlon, Inc.* the Delaware Court of Chancery, in voiding a so-called lock-up under which the directors of Revlon agreed to sell certain of Revlon's most valued assets to a favored bidder, noted particularly that the board "is composed of 14 directors."[7] Six of the directors are currently holding prominent positions in Revlon's management. Two of the remaining directors hold significant blocks of Revlon stock, and most of the non-management directors are or have been associated with entities doing business with Revlon.[8] On the other hand, the Federal District Court for the Southern District of New York, confronted with a similar situation, permitted the lock-up.[9] One of the principal bases on which it distinguished the Delaware decision in Revlon was the

[7]Fed. Sec. L. Rep. (CCH) ¶92,333 (Ct. Cer. Del., 1985), *aff'd* Del. Sup. Ct., Nov. 1, 1985.

[8]Id., at ¶92,217, n. 2.

[9]Hanson Trust PLC, et. al. v. SCM Corporation, et. al., slip. op. USDC, SDNY, 1985. Review of other grounds, F. 2d (20 C.R., 19). The Court of Appeals confirmed the finding of the district court with respect to the independence of a majority of the directors, but indicated that their independence did not relieve them of the responsibility to inform themselves about matters that come before them for determination.

fact that the board of SCM consisted principally of directors with
no other ties to SCM:

> The Court's findings of fact indicate that the nine independent direc-
> tors did not grant the lock-up options (or indeed take any action) out
> of self-interest, or bad faith, or fraud, or for any other improper pur-
> pose (such as attempting to entrench themselves or SCM's manage-
> ment in control). The three management directors did not vote on,
> and did not unduly influence the remaining directors in approving,
> either the Merrill Lynch $70.00 offer or the $74.00 offer and the lock-
> up options. The independent directors were precisely that: indepen-
> dent. They had no position in SCM's management, they did not own
> significant amount of SCM stock, they received no significant remuner-
> ation from SCM and they had no other meaningful business contact
> with SCM. Moreover, the independent directors did not act to per-
> petuate their positions on the SCM board, nor did they attempt to
> perpetuate the position of current SCM management. Thus, there has
> been no showing that the independent directors breached their duty
> of loyalty to SCM and its shareholders in any manner. Accordingly,
> the burden of proof to prove the fairness of the challenged transactions
> has not shifted to the SCM board.[10]

However, some dissenting judges have saddled outside directors as well as inside directors with the burdens of self-interest. In
the words of one,

> Directors of the New York Stock Exchange–listed companies are, at
> the very least, "interested" in their own positions of power, prestige
> and prominence (and in their not inconsequential perquisites). They
> are "interested" in defending against outside attack the management
> which they have, in fact, installed or maintained in power—"their"
> management (to which, in many cases, they owe their directorships).
> And they are "interested" in maintaining the public reputation of their
> own leadership and stewardship against the claims of "raiders" who
> claim they can do better.[11]

Notwithstanding such occasional dissents from the prevailing
disposition of courts to accord great importance to the independent

[10]Id., at 17.
[11]Papter v. Marshall Fields & Co., 646 F.2d 271 (7th Cir. 1981).

directors in the takeover situation, a company confronting an unwanted offer is well advised to accord the independent directors a major role in deciding the fairness of the offer and the measures to be taken to ward off the approach.

The role of the independent directors is not confined to action once a bid is taken or threatened. Increasingly companies, even before there is a hint of a possible bid, have adopted measures to hamper or make more costly and difficult an unnegotiated bid. The motives of insider directors in acting on such measures are equally suspect; hence the prudent course is to have them approved by the independent directors acting as a group or by a committee made up of independent directors. The matter should, of course, be approved by the full board, unless the committee of independent directors has been given the power to make a final determination (see Chapter 2).

OTHER SPECIAL COMMITTEES

At common law, contracts between a corporation and officers and directors were regarded as void. Most modern corporation laws provide that such contracts are valid and enforceable if they have been approved by disinterested directors. While some statutes would suggest that if there is such approval there is no need to inquire into the fairness of the contract or transaction, even in those states there is authority to the effect that if it appears that there has been a waste of corporate assets the court may set the contract aside regardless of the mode of approval. Thus, it is important that an appropriate inquiry be made by disinterested directors and that the inquiry include a determination that the contract is fair to the corporation.

Often, instead of a board's appointing a special committee to make such a determination, the disinterested directors as a group without formal constitution as a committee will make the necessary determination.

In addition to the committees discussed, boards will often find other situations in which it is desirable to use ad hoc committees to undertake inquiries, prepare special recommendations, or do one of a number of tasks. Such special committees, particularly when in sensitive situations outside directors are utilized, can be valuable mechanisms for conducting a corporation's business.

SUGGESTED REFERENCES

FERRERA, GERALD R., "Corporate Board Responsibility Under The Foreign Corrupt Practices Act of 1977," *American Business Law Journal*, 18 (1980), 259.

KENNEDY, THOMAS and CHARLES E. SIMON, *An Examination of Questionable Payments and Practices*. New York: Praeger, 1978.

Note, "Safe Harbors and Stormy Seas: Trends and Countertrends and Outside Director Liability," *Brooklyn Law Review*, 47 (1981), 259.

RING, MICHAEL, BRUCE C. SHERONY, and PHILLIPP A. STOEBERL, "The Impact of the Securities and Exchange Commission on Boards of Directors," *Directors Monthly*, National Association of Corporate Directors, Washington, D.C.: July/August 1986.

STEINBERG, MARC I., *Corporate Internal Affairs: A Corporate and Securities Law Perspective*. Westport, Conn.: Quorum Books, 1983.

STEINBERG, MARC I., "The Securities and Exchange Commission's Administrative, Enforcement, and Legislative Programs and Policies—Their Influence on Corporate Internal Affairs," *Notre Dame Law Review*, 58 (December 1982), 173.

10

REPORTING TO THE BOARD

DEFINITION AND IMPORTANCE OF COMMITTEE REPORTS

The end product of a standing committee's review of activities such as discussed in preceding chapters is an oral or written report to the full board of directors. The report usually consists of the standing committee's findings and recommendations, and its major objective is to provide to the full board information that will enable the board to develop and assess broad policy matters.

To help board committee members in their assessment of policy matters, it may be advisable to establish well in advance a two- to three-year annual-meeting calendar with meeting dates and proposed agenda items for all board committees. This will enable board committee members to reserve the committee dates. Furthermore, it should be emphasized that the standing committees serve not only the best interests of the stockholders because of the full board of directors' fiduciary responsibility to the stockholders, but also other board members who need comfort from a certain committee (e.g., audit committee) in discharging their stewardship accountability.

The reporting practices of the board's standing committees vary from company to company because there are no uniform standards of reporting. As a result, the format and wording of written reports will be different for each company. For example, the Conference Board found that with respect to the reporting practices of the audit committees:

> The customary method for the Audit Committee chairman to report to the full board was described by 606 companies. Half of the committee chairman give an oral report only; most of the remainder (264) add a written report to what they convey to the board orally.
>
> Two thirds of the 309 committees that submit minutes to the board do so only to keep the board informed; the board does not approve the minutes. In the remaining one-third of the committee that submit minutes, the board does have to approve them.[1]

[1]Jeremy Bacon, *Corporate Directorship Practices: The Audit Committee*, Report No. 766 (New York: The Conference Board, 1979), pp. 46–47.

In view of the American Bar Association Corporate Laws Committee's chapter 8 of its Revised Model Business Corporation Act, the standing committees of a board should give consideration to a formal written report. More specifically, a director who is not a member of the particular standing committee may rely on the information presented by the committee. Of course, the director who is relying on the information must act in good faith.[2]

Equally important, the board must remember that because of the separation of management and ownership of the company, a formal written report enables the board of directors through its standing committees to document its findings and recommendations. Such an approach allows the board to be more responsive at the annual stockholders' meeting. Accordingly, the need is for a formal written report that will convey to the full board the various economic, regulatory, social, and other potential issues affecting the company, and that will adequately inform the full board.

PREPARATION OF COMMITTEE REPORTS

In preparing effective committee reports for the board of directors, it is important to remember that committees act in an advisory capacity to the full board.[3] The content of the report should communicate this fact along with the committees' findings and recommendations. Of course, each committee should review its responsibility as disclosed in the company's bylaws or in the resolution of the board. Such a review enables each committee to develop a report within the province of its charge.

A committee report is the culmination of a committee's planning, review, evaluation, and follow-up activities. The objective of the report is to convey to the full board the scope of the committee's review and its formed opinions and recommendations.

Identifying and Securing Appropriate Sources of Information

In carrying out its responsibilities, each committee will consult with a number of different people. For example, the audit committee

[2]See Appendix D for further details.

[3]It should be noted that in Gall v. Exxon, the court recognized that a board committee had been given plenary power to act on its own authority.

will consult with the chief financial officer, the director of internal auditing, the external auditors, and, if necessary, outside consultants. As noted in the preceding chapters, standing committees operate part-time. Accordingly, each committee will rely on the expertise of selected individuals for direction and advice on how specific issues affect the company.

Each committee should request from the appropriate parties a concise executive summary of the major issues as disclosed in the supporting detailed reports. With respect to the committee's review strategy the chairman might consider such matters as a legal review of the reports, classified government material and commercial security information, and other confidential matters such as management succession and compensation. In addition, each report submitted to a committee should contain appropriate commentary that puts the committee on notice of important matters. For example, the author of a report should explain the reasons for a problem situation and the related course of action. This is particularly important to the committee because of the limitations of its members' time and resources.

Content of Committee Reports

During the report preparation phase, the chairperson of each committee will gather information. This information may consist of interim committee reports used to produce the annual committee report to the full board of directors. However, during the year the committee may wish to issue an interim committee report dealing with special matters so that such matters are reported to the board in a timely manner. This is particularly important with respect to matters (e.g., interim financial information) that require board attention and full board approval. The annual committee report is usually presented at the last meeting of the full board prior to the annual stockholders' meeting. Of course, during the full board's review and discussion with various committee chairpersons, the board may decide to incorporate certain information in the company's annual report, the annual Form 10-K Report submitted to the SEC, the company's pension plan report, and employee benefit plan reports.

In view of the fact that each committee will review various internal managerial reports, the content of these reports should be compared with the content of the committee's report to avoid any contradiction or misunderstandings between the representatives of management and the board of directors and its standing committees. In addition, the committee chairperson should use the "management by exception" principle to emphasize the problem areas that need the board's attention and corrective action. Typically, this information would be included in the executive summary of the committee report. The major objective is to provide a well-balanced committee report.

Although there is no universal standard of content and format for committee reports, an effective report should contain the following:

1. The title and date of the committee report (e.g., The Finance Committee Report, March 6, 1987).
2. The addressees of the report (i.e., the board of directors).
3. The jurisdictional charge of the committee. (The charge of the committee is disclosed in the corporate bylaws or board's resolution forming the committee.)
4. The scope of the committee's review (i.e., information concerning the extent of the committee's reviews, its activities and documents reviewed during the year).
5. A summary of the committee's activities for the year (i.e., agendas for and highlights of its meetings).
6. An executive summary of the committee's findings and recommendations.
7. Supplemental information (e.g., minutes of committee meetings).
8. The committee chairperson's signature and the identity of the other committee members.

Finally, an advantage of having a written formal committee report is that such information can be used to develop the narrative for the annual proxy statement. In particular, the SEC requires each registrant to disclose information relative to its nominating committee, compensation committee, and audit committee.

SUGGESTED REFERENCES

American Bar Association, *Corporate Director's Guide.* Chicago, Ill., 1978.

BACON, JEREMY, *Corporate Directorship Practices: The Audit Committee,* Report No. 766. New York: The Conference Board, Inc., 1979.

Korn/Ferry International, Board of Directors Twelfth Annual Study. New York: Korn/Ferry International, 1985.

CONCLUDING
OBSERVATIONS

Corporate board committees have a significant role in improving and maintaining the quality of corporate responsibility and accountability. As a result of the growing complexity of corporate entities and the industries in which they operate, board committees and full boards of directors continue to face change and challenge. Thus, to the extent that board committees can monitor activities related to corporate governance and understand the perceived needs of their outside constituencies, they can strengthen the full board's stewardship accountability.

Lester B. Korn and Richard M. Ferry, two executives of Korn/Ferry International, assert that

> ". . . directors are increasingly in the public spotlight, and they are going to be held more accountable for the actions of the corporations they serve."[1]

In view of this comment, this book clearly defines the role and responsibilities of board committees and explains how boards of directors through their standing committees can discharge their responsibilities to the stockholders and other outside constituencies most effectively.

---

[1]Korn/Ferry International, *Board of Directors Twelfth Annual Study* (New York: Korn/Ferry International, 1985), p. 1.

Foreign Corrupt Practices Act[1]

Be it enacted by the Senate and House of Representatives of the United States of America in Congress assembled,

Title I—Foreign Corrupt Practices

Short Title

Sec. 101. This title may be cited as the "Foreign Corrupt Practices Act of 1977."

Accounting Standards

Sec. 102. Section 13(b) of the Securities Exchange Act of 1934 (15 U.S.C. 78q(b)) is amended by inserting "(1)" after "(b)" and by adding at the end thereof of the following:

"(2) Every issuer which has a class of securities registered pursuant to section 12 of this title and every issuer which is required to file reports pursuant to section 15(d) of this title shall—

"(A) make and keep books, records, and accounts, which, in reasonable detail, accurately and fairly reflect the transactions and dispositions of the assets of the issuer; and

"(B) devise and maintain a system of internal accounting controls sufficient to provide reasonable assurances that—

[1]This act is contained in Title I of Public Law No. 95–213, December 19, 1977.

"(i) transactions are executed in accordance with management's general or specific authorization;

"(ii) transactions are recorded as necessary (I) to permit preparation of financial statements in conformity with generally accepted accounting principles or any other criteria applicable to such statements, and (II) to maintain accountability for assets;

"(iii) access to assets is permitted only in accordance with management's general or specific authorization, and

"(iv) the recorded accountability for assets is compared with the existing assets at reasonable intervals and appropriate action is taken with respect to any differences.

"(3) (A) With respect to matters concerning the national security of the United States, no duty or liability under paragraph (2) of this subsection shall be imposed upon any person acting in cooperation with the head of any Federal department or agency responsible for such matters if such act in cooperation with such head of a department or agency as done upon the specific, written directive of the head of such department or agency pursuant to Presidential authority to issue such directives. Each directive issued under this paragraph shall set forth the specific facts and circumstances with respect to which the provisions of this paragraph are to be invoked. Each such directive shall, unless renewed in writing, expire one year after the date of issuance.

"(B) Each head of a Federal department or agency of the United States who issues a directive pursuant to this paragraph shall maintain a complete file of all such directives and shall, on October 1 of each year, transmit a summary of matters covered by such directives in force at any time during the previous year to the Permanent Select Committee on Intelligence of the House of Representatives and the Select Committee on Intelligence of the Senate.

Foreign Corrupt Practices by Issuers

Sec. 103. (a) The Securities Exchange Act of 1934 is amended by inserting after section 30 the following new section:

Foreign Corrupt Practices by Issuers

"Sec. 30A. (a) It shall be unlawful for any issuer which has a class of securities registered pursuant to section 12 of this title or which is required to file reports under section 15 (d) of this title, or for any officer, director, employee, or agent of such (issuer or any stockholder thereof acting on behalf of such) issuer, to make use of the mails or any means or instrumentality of interstate commerce corruptly in furtherance of an offer, payment, promise to pay, or authorization of the payment of any money, or offer, gift, promise to give, or authorization of the giving of anything of value to—

"(1) any foreign official for purposes of—

"(A) influencing any act or decision of such foreign official in his official capacity, including a decision to fail to perform his official functions; or

"(B) inducing such foreign official to use his influences with a foreign government or instrumentality thereof to affect or influence any act or decision of such government or instrumentality, in order to assist such issuer in obtaining or retaining business for or with, or directing business to, any person;

"(2) any foreign political party or official thereof or any candidate for foreign political office for purposes of—

"(A) influencing any act or decision of such party, official, or candidate in its or his official capacity, including a decision to fail to perform its or his official functions; or

"(B) inducing such party, official, or candidate to use its or his influence with a foreign government or instrumentality thereof to affect to influence any act or decision of such government or instrumentality,

in order to assist such issuer in obtaining or retaining business for or with, or directing business to, any person; or

"(3) any person, while knowing or having reason to know that all or a portion of such money or thing of value will be offered, given, or promised, directly or indirectly, to any foreign official, to any foreign political party or official thereof, or to any candidate for foreign political office, for purposes of—

"(A) influencing any act or decision of such foreign official, political party, party official, or candidate in his or its official capacity, including a decision to fail to perform his or its official functions; or

"(B) inducing such foreign official, political party, party official, or candidate to use his or its influence with a foreign government or instrumentality thereof to affect or influence any act or decision of such government or instrumentality, in order to assist such issuer in obtaining or retaining business for or with, or directing business to, any person.

"(b) As used in this section, the term 'foreign official' means any officer or employee of a foreign government or any department, agency, or instrumentality thereof, or any person acting in an official capacity for or on behalf of such government or department, agency, or instrumentality. Such term does not include any employee of a foreign government or any department, agency, or instrumentality thereof whose duties are essentially ministerial or clerical."

(b)(1) Section 32 (a) of the Securities Exchange Act of 1934 (15 U.S.C. 78ff(a)) is amended by inserting "(other than section 30A)" immediately after "title" the first place it appears.

(2) Section 32 of the Securities Exchange Act of 1934 (15 U.S.C. 78ff) is amended by adding at the end thereof the following new subsection:

"(c)(1) Any issuer which violates section 30A(a) of this title shall, upon conviction, be fined not more than $1,000,000.

"(2) Any officer or director of an issuer, or any stockholder acting on behalf of such issuer, who willfully violates section 30A(a) of this title shall, upon conviction, be fined not more than $10,000, or imprisoned not more than five years, or both.

"(3) Whenever an issuer is found to have violated section 30A(a) of this title, any employee or agent of such issuer who is a United States citizen, national, or resident or is otherwise subject to the jurisdiction of the United States (other than an officer, director, or stockholder of such issuer,) and who willfully carried out the act or practice constituting such violation shall, upon conviction, be fined not more than $10,000, or imprisoned not more than five years, or both.

"(4) Whenever a fine is imposed under paragraph (2) or (3) of this subsection upon any officer, director, stockholder, employee, or agent of an issuer, such find shall not be paid, directly or indirectly, by such issuer."

Foreign Corrupt Practices by Domestic Concerns

Sec. 104. (a) It shall be unlawful for any domestic concern, other than an issuer which is subject to section 30A of the Securities Exchange Act of 1934, or any officer, director, employee, or agent of such domestic concern, to make use of the mails or any means or instrumentality of interstate commerce corruptly in furtherance of an offer, payment, promise to pay, or authorization of the payment of any money, or offer, gift, promise to give, or authorization of the giving of anything of value to—

(1) any foreign official for purposes of—

(A) influencing any act or decision of such foreign official in his official capacity, including a decision to fail to perform his official functions; or

(B) inducing such foreign official to use his influence with a foreign government or instrumentality thereof to affect or influence any act or decision of such government or instrumentality, in order to assist such domestic concern in obtaining or retaining business for or with, or directing business to, any person;

(2) any foreign political party or official thereof or any candidate for foreign political office for purposes of—

(A) influencing any act or decision of such party, official, or candidate in its or his official capacity, including a decision to fail to perform its or his official functions; or

(B) inducing such party, officials, or candidates to use its or his influence with a foreign government or instrumentality thereof to affect or influence any act or decision of such government or instrumentality,

in order to assist such domestic concern in obtaining or retaining business for or with, or directing business to, any person; or

(3) any person, while knowing or having reason to know that all or a portion of such money or thing of value will be offered, given, or promised, directly or indirectly, to any foreign official, to any foreign political party or official thereof, or to any candidate for foreign political office, for purposes of—

(A) influencing any act or decision of such foreign official, political party, party official, or candidate in his or its official capacity, including a decision to fail to perform his or its official functions; or

(B) inducing such foreign official, political party, party official, or candidate to use his or its influence with a foreign government or instrumentality thereof to affect or influence any act or decision of such government or instrumentality, in order to assist such domestic concern in obtaining or retaining business for or with, or directing business to any person.

(b)(1)(A) Except as provided in subparagraph (B), any domestic concern which violates subsection (a) shall, upon conviction, be fined not more than $1,000,000.

(B) Any individual who is a domestic concern and who willfully violates subsection (a) shall, upon conviction, be fined not more than $10,000, or imprisoned not more than five years, or both.

(2) Any officer or director of a domestic concern, or stockholder acting on behalf of such domestic concern, who willfully violates subsection (a) shall, upon conviction, be fined not more than $10,000, or imprisoned not more than five years, or both.

(3) Whenever a domestic concern is found to have violated subsection (a) of this section, any employee or agent of such domestic concern who is a United States citizen, national, or resident or is otherwise subject to the jurisdiction of the United States (other than an officer, director, or stockholder acting on behalf of such domestic concern), and who willfully carried out the act or practice constituting such violation shall, upon conviction, be fined not more than $10,000, or imprisoned not more than five years, or both.

(4) Whenever a fine is imposed under paragraph (2) or (3) of this subsection upon any officer, director, stockholder, employee, or agent of a domestic concern, such fine shall not be paid, directly or indirectly, by such domestic concern.

(c) Whenever it appears to the Attorney General that any domestic concern, or officer, director, employee, agent, or stockholder thereof, is engaged, or is about to engage, in any act or practice constituting a violation of subsection (a) of this section, the Attorney General may, in his discretion, bring a civil action in an appropriate district court of the United States to enjoin such act or practice, and upon a proper showing a permanent or temporary injunction or a temporary restraining order shall be granted without bond.

(d) As used in this section:

(1) The term "domestic concern" means (A) any individual who is a citizen, national, or resident of the United States; or (B) any corporation, partnership, association, joint-stock company, business trust, unincorporated organization, or sole proprietorship which has its principal place of business in the United States, or which is organized under the law of a State of the United States or a territory, possession, or commonwealth of the United States.

(2) The term "foreign official" means any officer or employee of a foreign government or any department, agency, or instrumentality thereof, or any person acting in an official capacity for or on behalf of any such government or department, agency, or instrumentality. Such term does not include any employee of a foreign government or any department, agency, or instrumentality thereof whose duties are essentially ministerial or clerical.

(3) The term "interstate commerce" means trade, commerce, transportation, or communication among the several States, or between any foreign country and any State or between any State and any place or ship outside thereof. Such term includes the intrastate use of (A) a telephone or other interstate means of communication, or (B) any other interstate instrumentality.

B

Proactive Position on Corporate Accountability and Board Committee Structure[1]

A. Nominating Committees

A corollary to the importance of the independence and character of individual directors is that the functioning of a nominating committee, by which potential directors are selected, is in itself a key element of accountability. In my view, this committee could become the single most effective force in improving corporate governance because of its impact, over time, on the composition of the board and on the succession of management. Tom Murphy of General Motors put it this way,

> Our experience at General Motors is that the nominating committee has a distinct and entirely helpful role to play in corporate governance and that companies need not wait to establish such a committee until they are forced to do so.

The nominating committee can best serve its function if it is comprised entirely of nonmanagement directors, as the *Corporate Directors Guidebook* recommends—particularly if they are independent. The chief executive officer should not be a member of the nominating committee. But, the committee should consult with him on the formulation of its recommendations. Indeed, absent more fundamental problems, I cannot imagine nomination of an individual with whom the chairman and the chief executive do not have at least a basic compatability.

[1]Harold M. Williams, Chairman-Securities and Exchange Commission, "Corporate Accountability—One Year Later." Address presented at the Sixth Annual Securities Regulation Institute, San Diego, Calif., 1979, pp. 23–30.

In selecting nominees, the committee's focus must be on independence, an acquiring mind, the ability to work with others, and a frame of reference and experience which brings tangible strengths to the board and corporate deliberations. The board should be measured by its collective talents and strengths and not by stereo-typing individual board members. Each board member need not have met payroll. The committee should recognize the desirability of including among the board's membership directors from outside the business community who can bring a different set of experiences and perspectives to the board. Token or constituency directors are not, however, a constructive response; directors selected solely for the names they bear or the constituency which their nomination placates may well make little or no contribution other than to pontificate occasionally when discussion turns to their area of interest.

In looking for nominees, I would not suggest that the nominating committee ignore potential independent directors because they are known to present board members, are graduates of the same universities or members of the same clubs, or live in the same neighborhoods. The search for directors should not, however, be contained within these perimeters. A significant source of independent outside directors can be found among senior management of other companies. Historically, only the top officers of corporations were invited to become board members of other corporations; perhaps we need now to look somewhat more broadly for individuals with experience and knowledge who can make a contribution to the board. Accounting and law firms—other than those retained by the corporation—universities, other not-for-profit organizations, and the ranks of former members of government are also fertile sources.

The nominating committee's role in director selection should extend beyond the recruitment of potential director candidates. The point of my ideal board is not to devise a set of inflexible rules—with respect to director independence or any other aspect of board membership—which should be imposed on every corporation. In a particular corporation, the benefits to be derived from including a member of management or a supplier may outweigh the costs. The crux of the problem is to assure that decisions concerning board composition reflect a reasoned and thoughtful balancing of these costs against the benefits expected from a given directors' board service. In my judgment, the nominating committee is the body which should measure the costs and determine whether the benefits outweigh them.

The nominating committee should also take on the responsibility for reviewing the performance of the board, both individual board members and collectively, and of recommending to the board changes in its responsibilities, composition, size, committee structure, and compensation. The nominating committee should also review the composition and membership of each of the standing committees, the board and committee fee structure, director retirement policy, management personnel serving on other boards, and the membership of the proxy committee charged with voting management's solicited proxies at the shareholder meetings. It should also review all proxy comments received from shareholders which relate directly or indirectly to the board and its composition and duties. The nominating committee should consider reducing the size of the board below what may have been the tradition. Too large a board can interfere with its effectiveness and make it impossible for any member to contribute meaningfully to board deliberations.

Good decision making requires a size small enough that each director can interact and share ideas with his fellows.

B. Compensation Committees

Another committee which has an important contribution to make to strengthening accountability is the compensation committee. This committee should be the focal point for issues such as the level of executive compensation, the form in which that compensation is to be paid, the noncash perquisites executives are to receive, and the manner and extent to which compensation should be geared to performance. In that latter regard, the compensation committee has a more subtle role in corporate accountability than is typically recognized. When compensation turns on short term economic performance, for example, it provides added incentive for executives to perform against that measure, perhaps at the expense of longer term viability or broader issues of social responsibility. Corporate compensation systems need to assure that what is being measured and what is being rewarded conform to what the board actually expects of the corporation and its executives. The compensation committee can be the vehicle for incorporating those expectations into the compensation structure.

C. Audit Committees

I have reserved audit committees for final mention, not because I believe they are less significant, but because their importance has already become fairly well recognized. Although the American Institute of Certified Public Accountants recently concluded that it should not compel public companies to establish audit committees as a pre-condition to obtaining an independent auditor's certification, it reiterated its support for the audit committee concept. In addition, the Foreign Corrupt Practices Act, and the importance which it places on establishing mechanisms to insure that the company has a functioning system of internal accounting controls, has given added impetus to the audit committee movement.

Thus, at this point, the central task is to define the audit committee's responsibilities and enhance the quality of the committee's work. Ralph Ferrara, the Commission's General Counsel, put it this way in an address to the Southwestern Legal Foundation last May:

> When the Commission calls for audit committees, the call is for effective, responsible audit committees, and not merely non-functioning, albeit decorative, shells. Regrettably, a survey published in the Coopers & Lybrand Audit Committee Guide states that among responding corporations only 60% of audit committees choose the outside accountant and only 40% review the yearly audit before its release. The most common audit committee function—reviewing the auditor's management letter—was performed only in two-thirds of the corporations. Frankly, I do not know what the other so-called audit committees are doing, but the Coopers & Lybrand study does not suggest that the effort underway in the private sector is anywhere near the quality necessary to insure against preemptive federal action.

I would only add that, while a large part of the problem is undoubtedly that some audit committees are the decorative shells to which Mr. Ferrara referred, equal danger lies in overloading the committee with responsibilities tangential or unrelated to their primary one. While the nominating committee, as I have suggested, may be the proper vehicle for board examination of the board's structure and composition, the audit committee should be permitted to concentrate on working with the corporation's accountants, both internal and external. The importance and uniqueness of that function militate strongly against requiring audit committee members to direct their attentions to other duties.

Committees of the Board[1]

THE FINANCE COMMITTEE includes both employe and non-employe Directors and is responsible for the determination of financial policies and the management of financial affairs including matters such as capital requirements and dividend recommendations to the Board.

ROGER B. SMITH	HOWARD H. KEHRL
Chairman	F. JAMES McDONALD
JOHN T. CONNOR	THOMAS A. MURPHY
WALTER A. FALLON	EDMUND T. PRATT, JR.
CHARLES T. FISHER, III	JOHN G. SMALE
ROBERT S. HATFIELD	F. ALAN SMITH

THE EXECUTIVE COMMITTEE is composed entirely of employe Directors and is responsible for determining operating policies, including product plans and the need for capital expenditures.

F. JAMES McDONALD	HOWARD H. KEHRL
Chairman	F. ALAN SMITH
DONALD J. ATWOOD	ROGER B. SMITH
ALEXANDER A. CUNNINGHAM	

[1]General Motors Corporation, *1984 Annual Report*, p. 34.

THE AUDIT COMMITTEE, composed entirely of non-employe Directors, selects the independent public accountants annually in advance of the Annual Meeting of Stockholders and submits the selection for ratification at the Meeting. In addition, the Committee reviews the scope and results of the audits, the accounting principles being applied, the effectiveness of the internal controls, and, in its oversight role, assures that management fulfills its responsibilities in the preparation of the financial statements.

JOHN D. DEBUTTS	JOHN. J. HORAN
Chairman	W. EARLE MCLAUGHLIN
ANNE L. ARMSTRONG	LEON H. SULLIVAN
JAMES H. EVANS	CHARLES H. TOWNES
MARVIN L. GOLDBERGER	

THE NOMINATING COMMITTEE, composed entirely of non-employe Directors, conducts continuing studies of the size and composition of the Board of Directors and recommends candidates for membership

WALTER A. FALLON	JOHN D. DEBUTTS
Chairman	CHARLES T. FISHER, III
CATHERINE B. CLEARY	ROBERT S. HATFIELD
JOHN T. CONNOR	JOHN J. HORAN

THE BONUS AND SALARY COMMITTEE, composed entirely of non-employe Directors, reviews executive compensation plans and benefit programs and determines compensation of Corporate officers and other members of the management group.

JOHN T. CONNOR	CHARLES T. FISHER, III
Chairman	ROBERT S. HATFIELD
ANNE L. ARMSTRONG	RAYMOND H. HERZOG
JAMES H. EVANS	THOMAS A. MURPHY
WALTER A. FALLON	

THE PUBLIC POLICY COMMITTEE, composed entirely of non-employe Directors, inquires into every phase of Corporate activities that relate to public policy and makes appropriate recommendations to management or the full Board.

CATHERINE B. CLEARY	ROSS PEROT
Chairman	EDMUND T. PRATT, JR.
JOHN D. DEBUTTS	JOHN G. SMALE
MARVIN L.	LEON H. SULLIVAN
GOLDBERGER	CHARLES H. TOWNES

D

Revised Model Business Corporation Act—Chapter 8: Directors and Officers[1]

Subchapter A. Board of Directors

§8.01. Requirement for and Duties of Board of Directors.—

(a) Except as provided in subsection (c), each corporation must have a board of directors.

(b) All corporate powers shall be exercised by or under the authority of, and the business and affairs of the corporation managed under the direction of, its board of directors, subject to any limitation set forth in the articles of incorporation.

(c) A corporation having 50 or fewer shareholders may dispense with or limit the authority of a board of directors by describing in its articles of incorporation who will perform some or all of the duties of a board of directors.

§8.02. Qualifications of Directors.—

The articles of incorporation or bylaws may prescribe qualifications for directors. A director need not be a resident of this state or a shareholder of the corporation unless the articles of incorporation or bylaws so prescribe.

[1]Adopted by Committee on Corporate Laws, Section of Corporation, Banking and Business Law of the American Bar Association (Chicago, Ill.: American Bar Association, 1984). For the official comments and statutory cross-references, see *Law and Business*, published by Harcourt Brace Jovanovich.

§8.03. Number and Election of Directors.—

(a) A board of directors must consist of one or more individuals, with the number specified in or fixed in accordance with the articles of incorporation or bylaws.

(b) If a board of directors has power to fix or change the number of directors, the board may increase or decrease by 30 percent or less the number of directors last approved by the shareholders, but only the shareholders may increase or decrease by more than 30 percent the number of directors last approved by the shareholders.

(c) The articles of incorporation or bylaws may establish a variable range for the size of the board of directors by fixing a minimum and maximum number of directors. If a variable range is established, the number of directors may be fixed or changed from time to time, within the minimum and maximum, by the shareholders or the board of directors. After shares are issued, only the shareholders may change the range for the size of the board or change from a fixed to a variable-range size board or vice versa.

(d) Directors are elected at the first annual shareholders' meeting and at each annual meeting thereafter unless their terms are staggered under section 8.06.

§8.04. Election of Directors by Certain Classes of Shareholders.—

If the articles of incorporation authorize dividing the shares into classes, the articles may also authorize the election of all or a specified number of directors by the holders of one or more authorized classes of shares. A class (or classes) of shares entitled to elect one or more directors is a separate voting group for purposes of the election of directors.

§8.05. Terms of Directors Generally.—

(a) The terms of the initial directors of a corporation expire at the first shareholders' meeting at which directors are elected.

(b) The terms of all other directors expire at the next annual shareholders' meeting following their election unless their terms are staggered under section 8.06.

(c) A decrease in the number of directors does not shorten an incumbent director's term.

(d) The term of a director elected to fill a vacancy expires at the next shareholders' meeting at which directors are elected.

(e) Despite the expiration of a director's term, he continues to serve until his successor is elected and qualifies or until there is a decrease in the number of directors.

§8.06. Staggered Terms for Directors.—

If there are nine or more directors, the articles of incorporation may provide for staggering their terms by dividing the total number of directors into two or three groups, with each group containing one half or one-third of the total, as near as may be. In that event, the terms of directors in the first group expire at the first annual shareholders' meeting after their election, the terms of the second group expire at the second annual shareholders' meeting after their election, and the terms of the third group, if any, expire at the third annual shareholders' meeting after their election. At each annual shareholders' meeting held thereafter, directors shall be chosen for a term of two years or three years, as the case may be, to succeed those whose terms expire.

§8.07. Resignation of Directors.—

(a) A director may resign at any time by delivering written notice to the board of directors, its chairman, or to the corporation.

(b) A resignation is effective when the notice is delivered unless the notice specifies a later effective date.

§8.08. Removal of Directors by Shareholders.—

(a) The shareholders may remove one or more directors with or without cause unless the articles of incorporation provide that directors may be removed only for cause.

(b) If a director is elected by a voting group of shareholders, only the shareholders of that voting group may participate in the vote to remove him.

(c) If cumulative voting is authorized, a director may not be removed if the number of votes sufficient to elect him under cumulative voting is voted against his removal. If cumulative voting is not authorized, a director may be removed only if the number of votes cast to remove him exceeds the number of votes cast not to remove him.

(d) A director may be removed by the shareholders only at a meeting called for the purpose of removing him and the meeting notice must state that the purpose, or one of the purposes, of the meeting is removal of the director.

§8.09. Removal of Directors by Judicial Proceeding.—

(a) The [name or describe] court of the county where a corporation's principal office (or, if none in this state, its registered office) is located may remove a director of the corporation from office in a proceeding commenced either by the corporation or by its shareholders holding at least 10 percent of the outstanding shares of any class if the court finds that (1) the director engaged in fraudulent or dishonest conduct, or gross abuse of authority or discretion, with respect to the corporation and (2) removal is in the best interest of the corporation.

(b) The court that removes a director may bar the director from reelection for a period prescribed by the court.

(c) If shareholders commence a proceeding under subsection (a), they shall make the corporation a party defendant.

§8.10. Vacancy on Board.—

(a) Unless the articles of incorporation provide otherwise, if a vacancy occurs on a board of directors, including a vacancy resulting from an increase in the number of directors:

    (1) the shareholders may fill the vacancy;

    (2) the board of directors may fill the vacancy; or

    (3) if the directors remaining in office constitute fewer than a quorum of the board, they may fill the vacancy by the affirmative vote of a majority of all the directors remaining in office.

(b) If the vacant office was held by a director elected by a voting group of shareholders, only the holders of shares of that voting group are entitled to vote to fill the vacancy if it is filled by the shareholders.

(c) A vacancy that will occur at a specific later date (by reason of a resignation effective at a later date under section 8.07(b) or otherwise) may be filled before the vacancy occurs but the new director may not take office until the vacancy occurs.

§8.11. Compensation of Directors.—

Unless the articles of incorporation or bylaws provide otherwise, the board of directors may fix the compensation of directors.

Subchapter B. Meetings and Action of the Board

§ 8.20. Meetings.—

(a) The board of directors may hold regular or special meetings in or out of this state.

(b) Unless the articles of incorporation or bylaws provide otherwise, the board of directors may permit any or all directors to participate in a regular or special meeting by, or conduct the meeting through the use of, any means of communication by which all directors participating may simultaneously hear each other during the meeting. A director participating in a meeting by this means is deemed to be present in person at the meeting.

§8.21. Action Without Meeting.—

(a) Unless the articles of incorporation or bylaws provide otherwise, action required or permitted by this Act to be taken at a board of directors' meeting may be taken without a meeting if the action is taken by all members of the board. The action must be evidenced by one or more written consents describing the action taken, signed by each director, and included in the minutes or filed with the corporate records reflecting the action taken.

(b) Action taken under this section is effective when the last director signs the consent, unless the consent specifies a different effective date.

(c) A consent signed under this section has the effect of a meeting vote and may be described as such in any document.

§8.22. Notice of Meeting.—

(a) Unless the articles of incorporation or bylaws provide otherwise, regular meetings of the board of directors may be held without notice of the date, time, place, or purpose of the meeting.

(b) Unless the articles of incorporation or bylaws provide for a longer or shorter period, special meetings of the board of directors must be preceded by at least two days' notice of the date, time, and place of the meeting. The notice need not describe the purpose of the special meeting unless required by the articles of incorporation or bylaws.

§8.23. Waiver of Notice.—

(a) A director may waive any notice required by this Act, the articles of incorporation, or bylaws before or after the date and time stated in the notice. Except as provided by subsection (b), the waiver must be in writing, signed by the director entitled to the notice, and filed with the minutes or corporate records.

(b) A director's attendance at or participation in a meeting waives any required notice to him of the meeting unless the director at the beginning of the meeting (or promptly upon his arrival) objects to holding the meeting or transacting business at the meeting and does not thereafter vote for or assent to action taken at the meeting.

§8.24. Quorum and Voting.—

(a) Unless the articles of incorporation or bylaws require a greater number, a quorum of a board of directors consists of:

(1) a majority of the fixed number of directors if the corporation has a fixed board size; or

(2) a majority of the number of directors prescribed, or if no number is prescribed the number in office immediately before the meeting begins, if the corporation has a variable-range size board.

(b) The articles of incorporation or bylaws may authorize a quorum of a board of directors to consist of no fewer than one-third of the fixed or prescribed number of directors determined under subsection (a).

(c) If a quorum is present when a vote is taken, the affirmative vote of a majority of directors present is the act of the board of directors unless the articles of incorporation or bylaws require the vote of a greater number of directors.

(d) A director who is present at a meeting of the board of directors or a committee of the board of directors when corporate action is taken is deemed to have assented to the action taken unless: (1) he objects at the beginning of the meeting (or promptly upon his arrival) to holding it or transacting business at the meeting; (2) his dissent or abstention from the action taken is entered in the minutes of the meeting; or (3) he delivers written notice of his dissent or abstention to the presiding officer of the meeting before its adjournment or to the corporation immediately after adjournment of the meeting. The right of dissent or abstention is not available to a director who votes in favor of the action taken.

§8.25. Committees.—

(a) Unless the articles of incorporation or bylaws provide otherwise, a board of directors may create one or more committees and appoint members of the board of directors to serve on them. Each committee may have two or more members, who serve at the pleasure of the board of directors.

(b) The creation of a committee and appointment of members to it must be approved by the greater of (1) a majority of all the directors in office when the action is taken or (2) the number of directors required by the articles of incorporation or bylaws to take action under section 8.24.

(c) Sections 8.20 through 8.24, which govern meetings, action without meetings, notice and waiver of notice, and quorum and voting requirements of the board of directors, apply to committees and their members as well.

(d) To the extent specified by the board of directors or in the articles of incorporation or bylaws, each committee may exercise the authority of the board of directors under section 8.01.

(e) A committee may not, however:

(1) authorize distributions;

(2) approve or propose to shareholders action that this Act requires be approved by shareholders;

(3) fill vacancies on the board of directors or on any of its committees;

(4) amend articles of incorporation pursuant to section 10.02;

(5) adopt, amend, or repeal bylaws;

(6) approve a plan of merger not requiring shareholder approval;

(7) authorize or approve reacquisition of shares, except according to a formula or method prescribed by the board of directors; or

(8) authorize or approve the issuance or sale or contract for sale of shares, or determine the designation and relative rights, preferences, and limitations of a class or series of shares, except that the board of directors may authorize a committee (or a senior executive officer of the corporation) to do so within limits specifically prescribed by the board of directors.

(f) The creation of, delegation of authority to, or action by a committee does not alone constitute compliance by a director with the standards of conduct described in section 8.30.

Subchapter C.   Standards of Conduct

§ 8.30. General Standards for Directors.—

(a) A director shall discharge his duties as a director, including his duties as a member of a committee:

(1) in good faith;

(2) with the care an ordinarily prudent person in a like position would exercise under similar circumstances; and

(3) in a manner he reasonably believes to be in the best interests of the corporation.

(b) In discharging his duties a director is entitled to rely on information, opinions, reports, or statements, including financial statements and other financial data, if prepared or presented by:

(1) one or more officers or employees of the corporation whom the director reasonably believes to be reliable and competent in the matters presented

(2) legal counsel, public accountants, or other persons as to matters the director reasonably believes are within the person's professional or expert competence; or

(3) a committee of the board of directors of which he is not a member if the director reasonably believes the committee merits confidence.

(c) A director is not acting in good faith if he has knowledge concerning the matter in question that makes reliance otherwise permitted by subsection (b) unwarranted.

(d) A director is not liable for any action taken as a director, or any failure to take any action, if he performed the duties of his office in compliance with this section.

§8.31. Director Conflict of Interest.—

(a) A conflict of interest transaction is a transaction with the corporation in which a director of the corporation has a direct or indirect interest. A conflict of interest transaction is not voidable by the corporation solely because of the director's interest in the transaction if any one of the following is true:

(1) the material facts of the transaction and the director's interest were disclosed or known to the board of directors or a committee of the board of directors and the board of directors or committee authorized, approved, or ratified the transaction;

(2) the material facts of the transaction and the director's interest were disclosed or known to the shareholders entitled to vote and they authorized, approved, or ratified the transaction; or

(3) the transaction was fair to the corporation.

(b) For purposes of this section, a director of the corporation has an indirect interest in a transaction if (1) another entity in which he has a material financial interest or in which he is a general partner is a party to the transaction if another entity of which he is a director, officer, or trustee is a party to the transaction and the transaction is or should be considered by the board of directors of the corporation.

(c) For purposes of subsection (a)(1), a conflict of interest transaction is authorized, approved, or ratified if it receives the affirmative vote of a majority of the directors on the board of directors (or on the committee) who have direct or indirect interest in the transaction, but a transaction may not be authorized, approved, or ratified under this section by a single director. If a majority of the directors who have no direct or indirect interest in the transaction vote to authorize, approve, or ratify the transaction, a quorum is present for the purpose of taking action under this section. The presence of, or a vote cast by a director with a direct or indirect interest in the transaction does not affect the validity of any action taken under subsection (a)(1) if the transaction is otherwise authorized, approved, or ratified as provided in that subsection.

(d) For purposes of subsection (a)(2), a conflict of interest transaction is authorized, approved, or ratified if it receives the vote of a majority of the shares entitled to be counted under this subsection. Shares owned by or voted under the control of a director who has a direct or indirect interest in the transaction, and shares owned by or voted under the control of an entity described in subsection (b)(1), may not be counted in a vote of shareholders to determine whether to authorize, approve, or ratify a conflict of interest transaction under subsection (a)(2). The vote of those shares, however, is counted in determining whether the transaction is approved under other sections of this Act. A majority of the shares, whether or not present, that are entitled to be counted in a vote on the transaction under this subsection constitutes a quorum for the purpose of taking action under this section.

§8.32. Loans to Directors.—

(a) Except as provided by subsection (c), a corporation may not lend money to or guarantee the obligation of a director of the corporation unless:

(1) the particular loan or guarantee is approved by a majority of the votes represented by the outstanding voting shares of all classes, voting as a single voting group, except the votes of shares owned by or voted under the control of the benefited director; or

(2) the corporation's board of directors determines that the loan or guarantee

benefits the corporation and either approves the specific loan or guarantee or a general plan authorizing loans and guarantees.

(b) The fact that a loan or guarantee is made in violation of this section does not affect the borrower's liability on the loan.

(c) This section does not apply to loans and guarantees authorized by statute regulating any special class of corporations.

§8.33. Liability for Unlawful Distributions.—

(a) Unless he complies with the applicable standards of conduct described in section 8.30, a director who votes for or assents to a distribution made in violation of this Act or the articles of incorporation is personally liable to the corporation of this Act or the articles of incorporation is personally liable to the corporation for the amount of the distribution that exceeds what could have been distributed without violating this Act or the articles of incorporation.

(b) A director held liable for an unlawful distribution under subsection (a) is entitled to contribution:

(1) from every other director who voted for or assented to the distribution without complying with the applicable standards of conduct described in section 8.30; and

(2) from each shareholder for the amount the shareholder accepted knowing the distribution was made in violation of this Act or the articles of incorporation.

Subchapter D.   Officers

§8.40. Required Officers.—

(a) A corporation has the officers described in its bylaws or appointed by the board of directors in accordance with the bylaws.

(b) A duly appointed officer may appoint one or more officers or assistant officers if authorized by the bylaws or the board of directors.

(c) The bylaws or the board of directors shall delegate to one of the officers responsibility for preparing minutes of the directors' and shareholders' meetings and for authenticating records of the corporation.

(d) The same individual may simultaneously hold more than one office in a corporation.

§8.41. Duties of Officers.—

Each officer has the authority and shall perform the duties set forth in the bylaws or, to the extent consistent with the bylaws, the duties prescribed by the board of directors or by direction of an officer authorized by the board of directors to prescribe the duties of other officers.

§8.42. Standards of Conduct for Officers.—

(a) An officer with discretionary authority shall discharge his duties under that authority:

(1) in good faith;

(2) with the care an ordinarily prudent person in a like position would exercise under similar circumstances; and

(3) in a manner he reasonably believes to be in the best interests of the corporation.

(b) In discharging his duties an officer is entitled to rely on information, opinions, reports, or statements, including financial statements and other financial data, if prepared or presented by:

(1) one or more officers or employees of the corporation whom the officer reasonably believes to be reliable and competent in the matters presented; or

(2) legal counsel, public accountants, or other persons as to matters the officer reasonably believes are within the person's professional or expert competence.

(c) An officer is not acting in good faith if he has knowledge concerning the matter in question that makes reliance otherwise permitted by subsection (b) unwarranted.

(d) An officer is not liable for any action taken as an officer, or any failure to take any action, if he performed the duties of his office in compliance with this section.

§8.43. Resignation and Removal of Officers.—

(a) An officer may resign at any time by delivering notice to the corporation. A resignation is effective when the notice is delivered unless the notice specifies a later effective date. If a resignation is made effective at a later date and the corporation accepts the future effective date, its board of directors may fill the pending vacancy before the effective date if the board of directors provides that the successor does not take office until the effective date.

(b) A board of directors may remove any officer at any time with or without cause.

§8.44. Contract Rights of Officers.—

(a) The appointment of an officer does not itself create contract rights.

(b) An officer's removal does not affect the officer's contract rights, if any, with the corporation. An officer's resignation does not affect the corporation's contract rights, if any, with the officer.

Subchapter E.   Indemnification

§8.50. Subchapter Definitions.—In this subchapter:

(1) "Corporation" includes any domestic or foreign predecessor entity of a corporation in a merger or other transaction in which the predecessor's existence ceased upon consummation of the transaction.

(2) "Director" means an individual who is or was a director of a corporation or an individual who, while a director of a corporation, is or was serving at the corporation's request as a director, officer, partner, trustee, employee, or agent of another foreign or domestic corporation, partnership, joint venture, trust, employee benefit plan, or other enterprise. A director is considered to be serving an employee benefit plan at the corporation's request if his duties to the corporation also impose duties on, or otherwise involve services by, him to the plan or to the participants in or beneficiaries of the plan. "Director" includes, unless the context requires otherwise, the estate or personal representative of a director.

(3) "Expenses" include counsel fees.

(4) "Liability" means the obligation to pay a judgment, settlement, penalty, fine (including an excise tax assessed with respect to an employee benefit plan), or reasonable expenses incurred with respect to a proceeding.

(5) "Official capacity" means: (i) when used with respect to a director, the office of the director in a corporation; and (ii) when used with respect to an individual other than a director, as contemplated in section 8.56, the office in a corporation held by the officer or the employment or agency relationship undertaken by the employee or agent on behalf of the corporation. "Official capacity" does not include service for any other foreign or domestic corporation or any partnership, joint venture, trust, employee benefit plan, or other enterprise.

(6) "Party" includes an individual who was, is, or is threatened to be made a named defendant or respondent in a proceeding.

(7) "Proceeding" means any threatened, pending, or completed action, suit, or proceeding, whether civil, criminal, administrative, or investigative and whether formal or informal.

§8.51. Authority to Indemnify.—

(a) Except as provided in subsection (d), a corporation may indemnify an individual made a party to a proceeding because he is or was a director against liability incurred in the proceeding if:

(1) he conducted himself in good faith; and

(2) he reasonably believed:

(i) in the case of conduct in his official capacity with the corporation, that his conduct was in its best interests; and

(ii) in all other cases, that his conduct was at least not opposed to its best interests; and

(3) in the case of any criminal proceeding, he had no reasonable cause to believe his conduct was unlawful.

(b) A director's conduct with respect to an employee benefit plan for a purpose he reasonably believed to be in the intersests of the participants in and beneficiaries of the plan is conduct that satisfies the requirement of subsection (a)(2)(ii).

(c) The termination of a proceeding by judgment, order, settlement, conviction, or upon a plea of nolo contendere or its equivalent is not, of itself, determinative that the director did not meet the standard of conduct described in this section.

(d) A corporation may not indemnify a director under this section:

(1) in connection with a proceeding by or in the right of the corporation in which the director was adjudged liable to the corporation; or

(2) in connection with any other proceeding charging improper personal benefit to him, whether or not involving action in his official capacity, in which he was adjudged liable on the basis that personal benefit was improperly received by him.

(e) Indemnification permitted under this section in connection with a proceeding by or in the right of the corporation is limited to reasonable expenses incurred in connection with the proceeding.

(e) Indemnification permitted under this section in connection with a proceeding by or in the right of the corporation is limited to reasonable expenses incurred in connection with the proceeding.

§8.52. Mandatory Indemnification.—

Unless limited by its articles of incorporation, a corporation shall indemnify a director who was wholly successful, on the merits or otherwise, in the defense of any proceeding to which he was a party because he is or was a director of the corporation against reasonable expenses incurred by him in connection with the proceeding.

§8.53. Advance for Expenses.—

(a) A corporation may pay for or reimburse the reasonable expenses incurred by a director who is a party to a proceeding in advance of final disposition of the proceeding if:

(1) the director furnishes the corporation a written affirmation of his good faith belief that he has met the standard of conduct described in section 8.51;

(2) the director furnishes the corporation a written undertaking, executed personally or on his behalf, to repay the advance if it is ultimately determined that he did not meet the standard of conduct; and

(3) a determination is made that the facts then known to those making the determination would not preclude indemnification under this subchapter.

(b) The undertaking required by subsection (a)(2) must be an unlimited general obligation of the director but need not be secured and may be accepted without reference to financial ability to make repayment.

(c) Determinations and authorizations of payments under this section shall be made in the manner specified in section 8.55.

§8.54. Court-Ordered Indemnification.—

Unless a corporation's articles of incorporation provide otherwise, a director of the corporation who is a party to a proceeding may apply for indemnification to the court conducting the proceeding or to another court of competent jurisdiction. On receipt of an application, the court after giving any notice the court considers necessary may order indemnification if it determines:

(1) the director is entitled to mandatory indemnification under section 8.52, in which case the court shall also order the corporation to pay the director's reasonable expenses incurred to obtain court-ordered indemnification; or

(2) the director is fairly and reasonably entitled to indemnification in view of all the relevant circumstances, whether or not he met the standard of conduct set forth in section 8.51 or was adjudged liable as described in section 8.51(d), but if he was adjudged so liable his indemnification is limited to reasonable expenses incurred.

§8.55. Determination and Authorization of Indemnification.—

(a) A corporation may not indemnify a director under section 8.51 unless authorized in the specific case after a determination has been made that indemnification of the director is permissible in the circumstances because he has met the standard of conduct set forth in section 8.51.

(b) The determination shall be made:

(1) by the board of directors by majority vote of a quorum consisting of directors not at the time parties to the proceeding;

(2) if a quorum cannot be obtained under subdivision (1), by majority vote of a committee duly designated by the board of directors (in which designation directors who are parties may participate), consisting solely of two or more directors not at the time parties to the proceeding;

(3) by special legal counsel:

(i) selected by the board of directors or its committee in the manner prescribed in subdivision (1) or (2); or

(ii) if a quorum of the board of directors cannot be obtained under subdivision (1) and a committee cannot be designated under subdivision (2), selected by majority vote of the full board of directors (in which selection directors who are parties may participate); or

(4) by the shareholders, but shares owned by or voted under the control of directors who are at the time parties to the proceeding may not be voted on the determination.

(c) Authorization of indemnification and evaluation as to reasonableness of expenses shall be made in the same manner as the determination that indemnification is permissible, except that if the determination is made by special legal counsel, authorization of indemnification and evaluation as to reasonableness of expenses shall be made by those entitled under subsection (b)(3) to select counsel.

§8.56. Indemnification of Officers, Employees, and Agents.—

Unless a corporation's articles of incorporation provide otherwise:

(1) an officer of the corporation who is not a director is entitled to mandatory indemnification under section 8.52, and is entitled to apply for court-ordered indemnification under section 8.54, in each case to the same extent as a director;

(2) the corporation may indemnify and advance expenses under this subchapter to an officer, employee, or agent of the corporation who is not a director to the same extent as to a director; and

(3) a corporation may also indemnify and advance expenses to an officer, employee, or agent who is not a director to the extent, consistent with public policy, that may be provided by its articles of incorporation, bylaws, general or specific action of its board of directors, or contract.

§8.57. Insurance.—

A corporation may purchase and maintain insurance on behalf of an individual who is or was a director, officer, employee, or agent of the corporation, or who, while a director, officer, employee, or agent of the corporation, is or was serving at the request of the corporation as a director, officer, partner, trustee, employee, or agent of another foreign or domestic corporation, partnership, joint venture, trust, employee benefit plan, or other enterprise, against liability asserted against or incurred by him in that capacity or arising from his status as a director, officer, employee, or agent, whether or not the corporation would have power to indemnify him against the same liability under section 8.51 or 8.52.

§8.58. Application of Subchapter.—

(a) A provision treating a corporation's indemnification of or advance for expenses to directors that is contained in its articles of incorporation, bylaws, a resolution of its shareholders or board of directors, or in a contract or otherwise, is valid only if and to the extent the provision is consistent with this subchapter. If articles of incorporation limit indemnification or advance for expenses, indemnification and advance for expenses are valid only to the extent consistent with the articles.

(b) This subchapter does not limit a corporation's power to pay or reimburse expenses incurred by a director in connection with his appearance as a witness in a proceeding at a time when he has not been made a named defendant or respondent to the proceeding.

E

Section 182 of the Business Corporations Act—Ontario, Canada

182 (1) The directors of a corporation that is offering its securities to the public shall elect annually from among their number a committee to be known as the audit committee to be composed of not fewer than three directors, of whom a majority shall not be officers or employees of the corporation of an affiliate of the corporation, to hold office until the next annual meeting of the shareholders.

(2) The members of the audit committee shall elect a chairman from among their members.

(3) The corporation shall submit the financial statement to the audit committee for its review and the financial statement shall thereafter be submitted to the board of directors.

(4) The auditor has the right to appear before and be heard at any meeting of the audit committee and shall appear before the audit committee when required to do so by the committee.

(5) Upon the request of the auditor, the chairman of the audit committee shall convene a meeting of the committee to consider any matters the auditor believes should be brought to the attention of the directors of shareholders.

Business Conduct Guidelines[1]

A Letter from the Chairman

Thanks to you—and your predecessors at IBM—our company has an enviable reputation. People generally think of us as competent, successful and ethical.

These three qualities are related. Our adherence to strict ethical standards has contributed, in a very direct way, to both the professionalism of our company and our success in the marketplace. Over the years, we have emphasized again and again that every employee is expected to act in accordance with the highest standards of ethics. This is still true today. And it will be true tomorrow.

But while the need for ethical behavior remains clear, the definition of it may not always be so clear. We operate in a rapidly changing industry. And IBM itself is changing very dramatically the way it does business. For example, the IBM Personal Computer now makes it possible for employees to write software on their own time for sale to IBM. For an IBM employee to be, at the same time, a vendor to IBM—certainly that's a relationship we didn't anticipate just a few years ago. And there are many similar examples.

Consequently, we have prepared this revised edition of IBM's *Business Conduct Guidelines*. It takes a new look at the ethical responsibilities which IBM employees have to customers, competitors, suppliers and the company. This revision also tries to address the complex and changing relationships which you, as an IBM employee,

[1]International Business Machines Corporation, *Business Conduct Guidelines,* 1983, and addendum, 1985, pp. 13–19.

164

may have to deal with. I believe it will answer many questions that have arisen since the last edition was published.

However, please remember that no rule book can cover all possible situations. Nor can it foresee changes, in the industry or in society, which may still lie around the corner. This is a mutual process; we will do all we can to help with advice and counsel. But, in the end, you must apply these guidelines to the best of your ability in your own individual situation. We depend on you to do the right thing; right for both you and the company. It is no exaggeration to say that IBM's reputation is in your hands.

Your record in exercising good judgment has been exemplary. And it's why I am confident that IBM will continue to enjoy an outstanding reputation.

John R. Opel, *Chairman of the Board*

Introduction

The purpose of this booklet is to provide general guidance to you, as an IBM employee on some common ethical and legal issues. You may encounter them either on or off the job but in one way or another they will be related to IBM's business interests. *

Since *IBM Business Conduct Guidelines* was last published in 1977, there have been significant changes in the information processing industry. Selling through dealers and other channels of distribution has become commonplace. Personal computers and computer literacy are spreading rapidly. The variety of specialized companies within our industry is increasing. And there have been social changes such as the growth in the number of two-career households. These changes and others have given rise to new questions and considerations, many of which are discussed in these guidelines.

The booklet first addresses certain responsibilities you have toward IBM, including the protection of the company's assets.

Then it focuses on your obligations in conducting IBM's business with other persons and organizations.

Next, it deals with considerations that arise when you are on your own time, especially conflicts of interest.

Finally, it discusses competition law as it relates to IBM.

IBM has been publishing corporate business conduct guidelines such as these for many years. Many of the company's functional areas and its divisions and subsidiaries also publish procedures and guidelines that elaborate on some of the issues discussed in this booklet and address other issues as well. But not even this collection of publications can provide all the answers. If you have questions about the issues raised or the material contained in this booklet or in the other procedures and guidelines, you should consult your manager or IBM legal counsel.

Section II.   Conducting IBM's Business

Some General Standards

The organizations we in IBM deal with include traditional customers, prospects and suppliers. But other organizations continue to emerge in our industry. They include leasing companies, software houses, distributors, dealers, banks and other financial institutions, Value Added Remarketers, equipment manufacturers, maintenance companies, third-party programmers and many others who compete with, buy from or sell to IBM.

No matter what type of organization you are dealing with, however, you should always observe these general standards:

No misrepresentation. Don't make misrepresentations to anyone you deal with. If you believe the other person may have misunderstood you, correct any misunderstanding you find exists. Honesty is integral to ethical behavior, and trustworthiness is essential for good, lasting relationships.

Don't use IBM's size unfairly. Some legitimate advantages—such as economies that derive from large-scale buying, selling and servicing—accrue to IBM because of its size. But you should never use IBM's size itself to intimidate, threaten or slight another person or organization. It has been our practice not to throw our weight around in dealing with other companies or organizations or with the public.

Treating everyone equitably. Everyone you do business with is entitled to fair and even-handed treatment. This is true whether you are buying, selling or performing in any other capacity for IBM.

Do not extend to another business enterprise preferential treatment such as unauthorized services or contract terms. IBM, of course, responds to competition in bidding for government and other business. However, if the circumstances require modified terms, they must be specifically approved by management.

IBM extends appropriate terms to each type of customer. For example, distributors, dealers and end-users all purchase certain IBM equipment under different terms. But within each category, we strive to treat equally all similarly placed customers, that is, those who are procuring in similar quantities and circumstances.

You must treat all suppliers fairly. In deciding among competing suppliers, weigh all the facts impartially, whether you are in purchasing, a branch office or some other part of the business, and whether you are buying millions of parts or a single, small repair job.

Whether or not you directly influence decisions involving business transactions, you must avoid doing anything that might create the appearance that a customer or a supplier has "a friend at IBM" who exerts special influence on its behalf.

No reciprocal dealing. Seeking reciprocity is contrary to IBM policy and in some cases may even be unlawful. You may not do business with a supplier of goods or of services (a bank, for example) on condition that it agrees to use IBM products or services. Do not tell a prospective customer that IBM deserves the business because of our own purchases from his or her organization.

This does not mean we cannot be supplied by an IBM customer. It does mean that IBM's decision to use a supplier must be independent of that supplier's decision to use IBM products or services.

Fairness in the Field

If you represent IBM in a marketing or service activity, the company asks you to compete not just vigorously and effectively but fairly as well. Avoid the following practices:

Disparagement. IBM relies on one thing above all to sell what it has to offer: excellence. It has long been the company's policy to provide customers the best possible products and services. Sell them on their merits, not by disparaging competitors, their products or services. False or misleading statements are improper. Avoid innuendo as well: do not "knock" the competition in an indirect way. Don't make comparisons that unfairly cast the competitor in a bad light.

In short, stress the advantages of IBM, not the disadvantages of competitors. To do otherwise only invites disrespect from customers and complaints from competitors.

Premature disclosure. IBM usually does not disclose to a particular prospect or customer anything about unannounced offerings that has not already been disclosed generally.

There are exceptions to this nondisclosure practice. One is when the national interest is involved. Another is when a customer works with IBM to develop or test new products, programs, services or distribution plans. For these and other special situations there are specific procedures for you to follow, and appropriate authorization is required in each instance.

Selling against competitive orders. As a matter of practice, if a competitor already has a firm order from a customer for an application, we don't market IBM products or services for that application before the competitor has installed. However, this is a complicated subject. For example, it is often difficult to determine whether a firm order actually exists. Letters of intent, free trials, conditional agreements and the like usually are not firm orders. Unconditional contracts are. Generally speaking, if a firm order does not exist, an IBM marketing representative may sell. When a situation is unclear or if there is any doubt seek advice from your business practices or legal function.

Relations with Other Organizations

Many companies have more than one relationship with IBM. A distributor, for example, may be both a customer and a competitor of IBM. Other companies may be both competitors and suppliers. Some companies may even be suppliers, competitors, distributors and end-users of IBM products. This requires that in any dealings you have with another company, you understand the particular relationship involved.

Generally, you should deal with another organization in only one relationship at a time. If, for example, you are buying from the other company, don't try to sell at the same time. That could be a first step toward reciprocity or preferential treatment as described above. However innocently motivated, such a step should be avoided.

Business contracts with competitors. Be careful of your relationship with any competitor. It is inevitable that employees of IBM and its competitors will meet, talk and attend the same business meetings from time to time. Many types of contacts are perfectly acceptable when established procedures have been followed. These include sales to other companies in our industry; purchases from them; participation in approved joint bids, business shows and standards organizations and attendance at trade association functions. But even these require caution.

Prohibitions. In all contacts with competitors, the general rule is to avoid discussing such matters as pricing policy, terms and conditions, costs, inventories, product plans, market surveys or studies, production plans and, of course, any other proprietary or confidential information.

Collaboration or discussion with competitors on these subjects can be illegal. If a competitor raises any of them, even lightly or with apparent innocence, you should object, stop the discussion immediately, tell the competitor firmly that under no circumstances can you discuss these matters and, if necessary, leave the meeting.

In summary, dissociate yourself and IBM from participation in any possibly illegal activity with competitors; confine yourself to what is clearly proper and lawful. Also, report immediately to IBM legal counsel any incident associated with a prohibited subject.

Acquiring and Using Information About Others

In the normal course of doing business, you will acquire information about other companies—customers, prospects, suppliers, competitors or other organizations—including information about their employees. In itself, this is not unethical. Indeed, it can hardly be avoided. In fact, IBM quite properly gathers this kind of information for such purposes as extending credit and evaluating suppliers. The company also, quite properly, collects competitive information from a variety of publicly available sources and uses it to evaluate the relative merits of its own products, services and marketing methods. In collecting this kind of information, it is engaging in an activity that, in a competitive system, is necessary and proper.

Acquiring information. There are limits, however, on how information should be acquired and used, especially information about competitors. No company should, *through improper means*, acquire a competitor's trade secrets or other confidential information.

Industrial espionage—burglary, wire-tapping, stealing and so forth—is obviously wrong. So is hiring a competitor's employees to get confidential information or urging a competitor's employees or customers to disclose confidential data. IBM will not tolerate any employee's engaging in any form of questionable intelligence gathering.

Using information. You should also be sensitive to how you use information about other companies, which often includes information about individuals. Those other companies and individuals are rightly concerned about their reputations and privacy. Adverse information of no business use should not even be retained in your files. And what information you do retain should be treated with discretion. For example, it should be communicated or made available only to those within the company who have a legitimate need to know. Also, when appropriate, in light of its nature and purpose, such information should be presented in the aggregate or in some other way to keep the identities of individuals and organizations to a minimum.

Acquiring Information from Others and Using It

Other organizations, like IBM, have intellectual property they want to protect. So do individuals. And, also like IBM, they are sometimes willing to disclose their confidential information for a particular purpose. If you are on the receiving end of another party's information, however, it is important that you proceed with caution.

Information you believe is confidential. To avoid IBM's being accused of misappropriating or misusing someone's confidential information, there are certain steps you should take.

First, determine whether the information actually is confidential. This is simple enough if it is in written form and labeled confidential, or perhaps proprietary, restricted or the like, or if you are told that the information—written or oral—is confidential. If the classification is not evident but you still have some reason to believe that the information may be confidential, ask the other party.

The same precaution applies to oral information. If, before entering into a meeting or a conversation, you believe that you will hear information that might be considered confidential, you should first clearly establish in writing that it is not confidential and that its use is unrestricted.

Next, you must not receive another's confidential information without the written approval of an appropriate IBM executive. Furthermore, the actual receiving of such information must not take place until the terms of its use have been formally agreed to by IBM and the other party. That means a written agreement approved by IBM legal and, usually, patent counsel. Once another party's confidential information is legitimately in your hands, you must use, copy, distribute and disclose that information only in accordance with the terms of that agreement.

Acquiring software. One type of intellectual property that must be managed with care is software that we acquire from others, whether computer programs, data bases or related documentation. Software is often protected by a copyright or as a trade secret or confidential information. Before you accept software or sign a license agreement, you must follow established procedures.

Also, if you acquire software for your personally owned equipment, you should not copy any part of such software in any development work for IBM or, generally, bring such software onto IBM premises.

Bribes, Gifts and Entertainment

Gifts between employees of different companies range from widely distributed advertising novelties, which you may both give and receive, to bribes which unquestionably you may not. You may pay for and accept customary business amenities such as meals, provided the expenses involved are kept at a reasonable level. Also, it frequently is necessary for a supplier, including IBM, to provide education and executive briefings for customers. It's all right to accept or provide some services in connection with this type of activity. Transportation in IBM or supplier planes to and from company locations, for instance, and lodging and food at company facilities generally are all right, although IBM normally expects its employees to use commercial carriers and facilities.

In the case of gifts, services and entertainment, however, there is a point of unacceptability. The difficulty lies in determining where that point is, unless, of course, laws make that clear.

One way to approach this question is to recognize that the purpose of both gifts and entertainment in business is to create good will. If they do more than that and *unduly influence* the recipient or make that person feel *obligated* to "pay back" the other company by giving it business, then they are unacceptable.

IBM's gift and entertainment guidelines are designed to be well within what the company believes is generally acceptable.

Receiving. Neither you, nor any member of your family, may solicit or accept from a supplier money or a gift that may reasonably be construed as having any connection with IBM's business relationship. Gifts include not just material goods but services and discounts on personal purchases of goods and services.

If you are offered money or a gift, or if one arrives at your home or office, tell your manager right away. Appropriate arrangements will be made to return or dispose of what has been received, and the supplier will be reminded of IBM's gift policy.

You may, with your manager's approval, accept a gift from a customer when the gift is of nominal value and is customarily offered to others having a similar relationship with the customer. Also, the promotional premiums and discounts offered by transportation companies, hotels, auto rental agencies and restaurants may be accepted when they are offered to travelers generally, unless IBM has specified to the contrary. Since the nature of these offerings is always changing, however, with new promotional programs being introduced frequently, IBM's practices on what may be accepted are also subject to change. You should, therefore, consult with your manager if you have any doubts regarding a specific situation.

When authorized by IBM, marketing people may refer customers to third-party vendors such as Value Added Remarketers, third-party programmers or financing houses. However, IBMers may not accept from anyone, except IBM, any fee, commission or other compensation for this activity.

Giving. You may not give money or any gift to an executive, official or employee of any supplier, customer, government agency or other organization if it could reasonably be construed as having any connection with IBM's business relationship. In countries where local customs call for giving gifts on special occasions to customers and others, you may, with appropriate prior approval, proffer gifts that are lawful, appropriate in nature and nominal in value, provided this cannot be construed as seeking special favor.

Relationships with government employees. What is acceptable in the business world may not be acceptable and may even be strictly against regulations in dealings with government employees. Clearly, the relevant laws governing relations between government customers and suppliers must be adhered to.

G

Management's Financial Responsibility

Management is responsible for the preparation of the Company's financial statements and the other financial information in this report. This responsibility includes maintaining the integrity and objectivity of the financial records and the presentation of the Company's financial statements in accordance with generally accepted accounting principles.

The Company maintains a system of internal controls designed to provide reasonable assurance that its records include the transactions of its operations in all material respects and to provide protection against significant misuse or loss of Company assets. The internal control system is supported by a staff of internal auditors who employ thorough auditing programs, by careful selection and training of financial management personnel, and by written procedures that communicate the details of the control system to the Company's worldwide activities.

The Company's financial statements have been examined by Coopers & Lybrand, independent certified public accountants. Their examination was made in accordance with generally accepted auditing standards which included a reveiw of the internal control system and a test of transactions. The Auditors' Opinion appears on this page.

The Board of Directors, acting through its Audit Committee composed solely of directors who are not employees of the Company, is responsible for determining that management fulfills its responsibilities in the preparation of financial statements and the financial control of operations. The Audit Committee appoints the inde-

[1]Ford Motor Company, *1984 Annual Report*, p. 36.

pendent public accountants subject to ratification by the stockholders. It meets regularly with management, internal auditors and independent accountants. The independent accountants have full and free access to the Audit Committee and meet with it to discuss their audit work, the Company's internal controls and financial reporting matters.

H

Business or Professional Organizations and Directors Publications

American Bar Association
750 N. Lake Shore Drive
Chicago, IL 60611

American Institute of Certified Public
Accountants
1211 Avenue of the Americas
New York, NY 10036

American Law Institute
4025 Chestnut Street
Philadelphia, PA 19104

American Society of Corporate
Secretaries, Inc.
One Rockefeller Plaza
New York, NY 10020

The Business Roundtable
200 Park Avenue
New York, NY 10166

The Conference Board
845 Third Avenue
New York, NY 10022

The Corporate Board
1210 South Shenandoah
#303
Los Angeles, CA 90035

Directors & Boards
229 South 18th Street
Philadelphia, PA 19103

Directorship
Directors Publications, Inc.
181 Post Road West
P.O. Box 5198
Westport, CT 06881

Financial Accounting Standards Board
High Ridge Park
Stamford, CT 06905

Financial Analysts Federation
1633 Broadway
New York, NY 10019

Financial Executives Institute
10 Madison Avenue
Morristown, NJ 07960

Heidrick and Struggles
245 Park Avenue
New York, NY 10167

The Institute of Internal Auditors, Inc.
249 Maitland Avenue
Altamonte Springs, FL 32701

Institute of Management Accounting
570 City Center Building
Ann Arbor, MI 48104

Korn/Ferry International
277 Park Avenue
New York, NY 10172

National Association of Accountants
919 Third Avenue
New York, NY 10022

National Association of Corporate
  Directors
450 5th Street, N.W.
Securities & Exchange Commission
  Building
Suite 1110
Washington, D.C. 20001

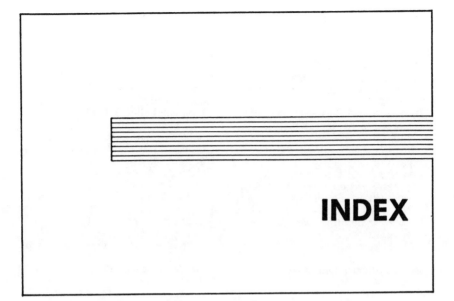

INDEX

Accountability, corporate, 7, 145–48
Accounting controls, internal, 30–31, 103–7
Accounting Establishment, The, 14
Accounting profession, 13–14, 97
Acquisition committees, 122–25
Acquisitions, 16–17
American Bar Association, 7
  address of, 177
  Committee on Corporate Laws, 24, 46, 57, 63, 130, 151
  Corporate Directors' Guidebook of, 14–15, 145
  Revised Model Business Corporations Act of, 23–24, 27–28, 130, 151–63
American Institute of Certified Public Accountants (AICPA), 7
  address of, 177
  audit committees and, 98–100, 104, 147
American Law Institute, 16, 120–21, 177
American Society of Corporate Secretaries, Inc., 177
American Stock Exchange corporations, 63, 64, 70, 97, 100

Ancillary relief, 113–14
Appointment of committees, 28–29
  power of the board and, 25–28
Audit committees, 8, 15, 16, 29, 92, 97–108
  corporate accountability and, 147–48
  follow-up meetings, 107–8
  of Ford Motor Company, 175–76
  of General Motors Corporation, 150
  historical development, 97–98
  organization of, 98–101
  planning meetings, 102–4
  reporting practices of, 129
  review and evaluation meetings, 105–7
Auditing:
  external, 102–3
  internal, 30–31, 103–7
  (*see also* Audit committees)

Board committee law, 23–34
  appointment of committees, 28–29
  duties of committee members, 32–34
  executive committees and, 26, 33, 42

Board committee law (cont.)
  general principles, 23–25
  power to appoint committees, 25–28
  reliance by non-committee members,
    29–32
  Revised Model Business
    Corporations Act, 23–24, 27–28,
    130, 151–63
Board committees, 10, 12, 14–16, 137
  reports of, 129–32
  (see also Audit committees; Com-
    pensation committees; Executive
    committees; Finance committees;
    Nominating committees; Public-
    policy committees; Special
    committees)
Board of directors:
  reports to, 129–32
  (see also Board committees;
    Corporate law)
Brown, Courtney, 55
Business Conduct Guidelines (IBM
  Corporation), 167–73
Business Corporations Act—Ontario,
  Canada, 97, 165
Business judgment rule, 17, 24–25,
  120
Business organizations, addresses of,
  177–78
Business Roundtable, The, 7, 14–16,
  46, 58, 63, 177
Business Week, 14

Caplin, Mortimer, 43
Care, duty of, 12, 13, 23–24, 28–29,
  33–34
Changing Board, The (Heidrick and
  Struggles), 49
Charters, corporate, 3–4, 11
Chief executive officer, 50–51, 54–55,
  57–58, 65
Chief financial officer, 87, 90–91
Clayton Act, 53–54
Committee reports, 129–32
Committees (see Board committees)
Common law, 3
Company needs, nominations and,
  52, 53
Compensation committees, 10, 63–73
  benefits of, 63, 65–66
  corporate accountability and, 147
  of General Motors Corporation, 150
  historical development, 63, 64
  illustrative discussion of executive
    compensation, 69, 71–73
  profile of, 64
  task of, 66–70

Conference Board, The, 101, 129, 177
Confidentiality, 117
Conflicts of interest, 53
Congress, 11–14, 99
Consent order, 114
Continental Illinois Bank, 121
"Cooked books" charges, 117
Coopers & Lybrand, 147, 175
Corporate accountability, 7, 145–48
Corporate Board, The, 177
Corporate charters, 3–4, 11
Corporate Directors' Guidebook,
  14–15, 145
Corporate law:
  acquisitions and, 16–17
  Congress and, 11–14
  corporate community concern with,
    14–16
  of Delaware, 4, 17, 18, 25, 119–20
  Foreign Corrupt Practices Act, 7,
    11, 30–31, 98, 99, 139–43, 147
  historical development, 3–6
  liability insurance and, 17–18
  litigation committees, 118–21
  Securities Act of 1933, 5–6, 31–32
  Securities and Exchange Com-
    mission and, 7–10
  Watergate affair and, 6–7, 11, 13
  (see also Board committee law)
Counsel, 117
Court actions, 113–14, 119–20,
  123–25

Delaware, 4, 17, 18, 25, 119–20
Diligence, duty of, 31–32
Directors & Boards, 177
Directorship, 177
Directors Publications, Inc., 177–78
Disclosure requirements, 9, 10
District courts, 113–14, 119, 123–24
Due care, 17, 30–31
Duties:
  of board committees, 13
  of committee members, 32–34
  of directors, 12, 13, 23–24, 28–29

Escott v. BarChris Construction
  Corp. (1968), 31–32
Executive Alert Newsletter, 69,
  71–72
Executive committees, 26, 33, 39–46
  advantages of, 40–42
  of General Motors Corporation, 149
  guidelines for establishing, 44–46
  historical development, 39–40
  typical functions of, 42–44
Executive succession, 54–55
Exxon Corporation, 119

Federal Trade Commission, 53–54
Ferrara, Ralph, 147
Ferry, Richard M., 137
Finance committees, 87–94
    basic functions of, 90–94
    basic structure of, 88–90
    of General Motors Corporation, 149
    historical development, 87
    need for, 88
Financial Accounting Standards Board
    (FASB), 92–93, 177
Financial Analysts Federation, 178
Financial Executives Institute, 178
Financial responsibility of manage-
    ment, 175–76
Forbes, 14
Ford Motor Company, 175–76
Foreign Corrupt Practices Act of
    1977, 7, 11, 30–31, 98, 99,
    139–43, 147
Form 10-K report, 103, 105, 131

Gall v. Exxon (1976), 119
Geneen, Harold, 10
General corporation laws, 4
General Electric Company, 68, 87,
    100–101
General Motors Corporation, 49, 77,
    78, 149–50
*General Motors Public Interest Report
    1984*, 81, 82

Harvard Business Review, 14
Heidrick and Struggles, 49, 66, 67,
    77, 87, 178
Hills, Roderick M., 15
Holding companies, 4

IBM Corporation, 167-73
Institute of Internal Auditors, Inc.,
    106, 178
Institute of Management Accounting,
    178
Internal accounting controls, 30–31,
    103-7
Investigating committees, 121–22

Jaw-boning, 9–10

Karmel, Roberta, 49
Killearn Properties, Inc., 98
Korn/Ferry International, 39, 43, 63,
    66–68, 79, 137, 178

Law (*see* Board committee law;
    Corporate law)
Liability:
    of committee members, 32–34

for misleading financial statements,
    88
of non-committee directors, 29–32
Liability insurance, 17–18, 58
Litigation committees, 118–21
Loyalty, duty of, 12, 13, 24, 29
Lums, Inc., 98

*MacAndrews & Forbes Holdings,
    Inc. v. Reston, Inc.* (1985),
    123–24
Marshall Field & Company, 17
Mattel, Inc., 98
Metcalf, Lee, 13–14
Metzenbaum, Howard, 11–13, 54,
    100
Minority groups, nominations and, 52
Moss, John, 14, 99
Murphy, Thomas A., 49, 145

Nader, Ralph, 11
National Association of Accountants,
    178
National Association of Corporate
    Directors, 178
New York Stock Exchange (NYSE), 7,
    15–16, 29, 63, 64, 70, 97–99
Nominating committees, 10, 13, 15,
    49–58
    corporate accountability and,
    145–47
    of General Motors Corporation, 150
    historical development, 49
    importance of, 49–51
    responsibilities of, 51–58
Non-committee members, reliance by,
    29–32

Opel, John R., 168
Over-the-counter companies, 63, 64,
    70

Palmer, Russell E., 94
Penn Central Company, 7–8, 98
Professional organizations, addresses
    of, 177–78
Protection of Shareholders Rights Act
    of 1980, 100
Proxy rules, SEC, 52, 99
Public-policy committees, 77–83
    of General Motors Corporation, 150
    historical development, 77
    operational aspects of, 79–83
    significance of, 77–79

Report on Oversight Committees, 46
Reports, committee, 129–32

Revised Model Business Corporations
    Act of 1984, 23–24, 27–28, 130,
    151–63
*Role and Composition of the Board
    of Directors of the Large Publicly
    Owned Corporation, The*, 14,
    46, 58
Rosenthal, Benjamin, 11–12

SCM Corporation, 123*n*, 124
Securities Act of 1933, 5–6, 31–32
Securities and Exchange Commission
    (SEC), 6–10, 14, 92
  address of, 178
  audit committees and, 8, 97–100
  compensation committees and, 63,
    65–67, 71
  "corporate Watergate" and, 6
  executive committees and, 43–44
  nominating committees and, 10,
    51, 52
  role in corporate governance, 7–10
  special committees and, 113–15,
    117, 122
Securities Exchange Act of 1934, 6
Senate Committee on Governmental
    Affairs, Metcalf Subcommittee on
    Reports, Accounting and
    Management of, 99

Shad, John S. R., 16
Shapiro, Irving S., 69, 71–72
Shareholder litigation, 118–21
Sherman Antitrust Act, 5
Smith, Bryan, 66
Smith v. Van Gorkom (1985), 16, 25
Social responsibility, 77–79
Special committees, 113–25
  acquisition committees, 122–25
  effectiveness of, 116–17
  historical development, 113–16
  investigating committees, 121–22
  litigation committees, 118–21
  other committees, 125
  purposes of, 116
Sporkin, Stanley, 8
Standard Oil Company, 5
*Standards for the Professional
    Practice of Internal Auditing*,
    107

Taming the Giant Corporation
    (Nader et al.), 11
Task Force on Corporate Account-
    ability, 10
Telephonic board meetings, 40

Watergate affair, 6–7, 11, 13
Williams, Harold M., 10, 65–66,
    145–48